T0268800

MARVELOUSLY
REVOLTING
RECIPES

VIKING
An imprint of Penguin Random House LLC, New York

First published in the United Kingdom by Penguin UK, 2023
First published in the United States of America by Viking,
an imprint of Penguin Random House LLC, 2024
Some recipes previously published by Puffin Books, 1994, 2001, 2009
This edition with new and previous recipes, first published in the United Kingdom, 2023

Text copyright © The Roald Dahl Story Company Ltd, 2023
Food photography by Jan Baldwin
Illustrations by Quentin Blake, Abe Odedina, Alex Scarfe, Alexis Deacon, Axel Scheffler, Chris Riddell,
Chris Wormell, Diane Ewen, Emily Woodard, Emma Chichester Clark, Ian Beck, Joel Stewart,
Lane Smith, Lauren O'Hara, Mini Grey, Rikin Parekh, Steven Lenton, Tim Stevens
Illustrations on pages 10 and 11, 26 and 27, 30–33, 36 and 37, 38 and 39, 42 and 43,
68 and 69, 78 and 79, copyright © Quentin Blake, 1993, 2001, 2009
All other illustrations © Abe Odedina, Alex Scarfe, Alexis Deacon, Axel Scheffler, Chris Riddell,
Chris Wormell, Diane Ewen, Emily Woodard, Emma Chichester Clark, Ian Beck, Joel Stewart,
Lane Smith, Lauren O'Hara, Mini Grey, Rikin Parekh, Steven Lenton, Tim Stevens, 2023
Photo of Joanna Lumley © Rankin
Photo of Quentin Blake © Linda Kitson
Illustrations to accompany additional information on pages 90–120 (and placed elsewhere
throughout the book) by Laura Coppolaro for The Roald Dahl Story Company.
The brands mentioned in this book are trademarks belonging to third parties.
Recipe text by Lori Newman
"Monkey Bark" recipe by Hannah Summers
Photo on p. iv © Hannah Summers
With thanks to Sonali Shah for contributions to the guides.

Penguin supports copyright. Copyright fuels creativity, encourages diverse voices, promotes free
speech, and creates a vibrant culture. Thank you for buying an authorized edition of this book and
for complying with copyright laws by not reproducing, scanning, or distributing any part of it in
any form without permission. You are supporting writers and allowing Penguin to continue to
publish books for every reader.

Viking & colophon are registered trademarks of Penguin Random House LLC.
The Penguin colophon is a registered trademark of Penguin Books Limited.

Visit us online at PenguinRandomHouse.com.

Library of Congress Cataloging-in-Publication Data is available.

ISBN 9780593525012
1 3 5 7 9 10 8 6 4 2

Manufactured in China
TOPL

Design by Katy Finch
Text set in Aleo, Futura, and Roald Dahl Wonky

The publisher does not have any control over and does not assume any responsibility for author or
third-party websites or their content.

INSPIRED BY THE STORIES OF

ROALD DAHL

MARVELOUSLY

REVOLTING
RECIPES

VIKING

Books by Roald Dahl

THE BFG

BILLY AND THE MINPINS

BOY: TALES OF CHILDHOOD

CHARLIE AND THE CHOCOLATE FACTORY

CHARLIE AND THE GREAT GLASS ELEVATOR

THE COMPLETE ADVENTURES OF CHARLIE
AND MR. WILLY WONKA

DANNY THE CHAMPION OF THE WORLD

DIRTY BEASTS

THE ENORMOUS CROCODILE

ESIO TROT

FANTASTIC MR. FOX

GEORGE'S MARVELOUS MEDICINE

THE GIRAFFE AND THE PELLY AND ME

GOING SOLO

JAMES AND THE GIANT PEACH

THE MAGIC FINGER

MARVELOUSLY REVOLTING RECIPES

MATILDA

THE MISSING GOLDEN TICKET AND OTHER SPLENDIFEROUS SECRETS

THE TWITS

THE VICAR OF NIBBLESWICKE

THE WITCHES

THE WONDERFUL STORY OF HENRY SUGAR AND SIX MORE

To discover more books, and find out more about
Roald Dahl, please visit the website at **RoaldDahl.com.**

A photograph of Felicity Dahl's mother, Elizabeth Throckmorton, who was an inspiration for creating the Roald Dahl Pediatric Nurses

For all Marvellous Roald Dahl Nurses

To-day we have a cooking class. . . .

A drawing by Elizabeth Throckmorton

CONTENTS

ON FEASTS

A FOREWORD BY SOPHIE DAHL

I called him Mold, because when I was a toddler they tried to teach me to say the Norwegian pronunciation of his name, "Roo–al," but my baby tongue couldn't get to grips with it at all. He was Mold from then on, sometimes Moldy, which suited him, with his creaky frame and voice like a bonfire.

Like all good magicians, Mold had a vast supply of tricks up his sleeve, conjured from the everyday. Amaretto biscuits whose paper you lit and which shot up into the sky like titchy hot-air balloons, falling back to Earth in a wispy question mark of ash. A miniature steam train that huffed and puffed around the dining room table if you filled it with water. Weedkiller that spelled out our names in the grass in the night, because the fairies had paid a visit. Mold's windows were dotted with Witch Balls: ancient, candy-colored spheres, employed to ward off any witches, should they appear at the glass.

At his table, a meal was never simply a meal. It was another opportunity for a story, a tall tale to soften the various injustices involved in being a child.

On bacon and marmalade sandwiches: "I got this recipe from a prince in Dar es Salaam; I saved him from the jaws of a python, and in exchange he gave me this exquisite combination."

French onion soup: "A nun in Burgundy served me this; a Mother Superior who smuggled ice cream in her bloomers in the war. She didn't flinch as it melted down her legs."

Mold understood that going back to boarding school aged ten was tough, that the memory of the supper you'd get the night before would keep you going for weeks when you were homesick. He'd been there himself. Roast chicken and roast potatoes? Done. Cream of tomato soup? Of course. Chocolate bombe? Tick. With extra cream, please.

The Red Tupperware Box that appeared at his house at the end of every lunch and dinner heralded the most important and longed-for bit of the meal. Its functionality belied the glory of what lay inside. If you had been good at the table, you could collect it from the kitchen and bring it to the dining room while the grown-ups were having their coffee. The Box contained chocolate. Lots of it, in appealing child-sized bars, nothing fancy but always compelling. Flake, Toblerone, Aero, Curly Wurly, Kit Kat. An exotic Scandinavian concoction, which Mold handed over after a book tour in Sweden, the smooth-on-the-outside, crunchy-on-the-inside Daim bar. Heaven-sent. Maltesers, Rolo, Crunchie, Yorkie. We knew the dates and history of each bar. Together we explored that Tupperware like a pair of archaeologists on a quest for the ultimate bite.

Mold died when I was thirteen years old. He would be over the moon that today children are making recipes inspired by his characters and that the Marvellous Children's Charity and its heroes walk alongside the BFG and the Enormous Crocodile in this book. Like his beloved widow, Liccy, Mold knew firsthand the devastating impact of sick children and had the utmost respect for those that cared for them.

Now it's your turn for sweet imaginings and flights of fancy. For Fizzwinkles, Swudge, and Dandyprats. Onward with the feast!

AN INTRODUCTION
BY FELICITY DAHL

I am often asked which is my favorite book by Roald Dahl, and my answer is always *James and the Giant Peach*. "Why?" you may ask. Well, one of the most important things in life is the choice of your friends, and James of course made a great choice. His friends helped him make the perfect escape from the awful Aunt Spiker and Aunt Sponge. They were intrepid. They crossed an ocean to get as far away as possible from those beastly aunts. But they also needed food, and the peach provided this. "There's nothing like it! There never has been!" the centipede declares at one point in the book. And he should know—he has tasted all the finest foods in the world. His song about all the exotic and eccentric food he likes to eat has inspired many of the revolting recipes in this book.

Like the centipede in *James*, Roald was fascinated by food. Of all shapes and sizes. One of his first letters home from boarding school, written at age nine, describes his fascination at how an owl can eat a mouse whole, skin and bones and everything.

I don't think Roald ever ate a mouse, but in his own life he was always adventurous—wanting to try new things. He learned to cook at an early age in order to supplement the disgusting school meals he was given. His dear mother would send him exciting food parcels containing raw eggs.

This book has not been put together by a centipede, but by Lori Newman, who is a wonderful and original cook. The recipes are inspired by the wonderful and wondrous foods that are featured in the books of Roald Dahl. From Willy Wonka's Hair Cream to the BFG's beautiful Magic Mixed Dream, it is a collection full of tasty and exciting dishes. You (or maybe the adults in your life) may remember three previous Revolting Recipes books that have been published over the last thirty years or so. Although this book contains a host of new recipes, there are some old favorites included here and there—illustrated by the marvelous Sir Quentin Blake.

I hope the recipes in this book are both fun and relatively easy to make and that they will be even stranger and more scrumptious than the ones the centipede celebrates.

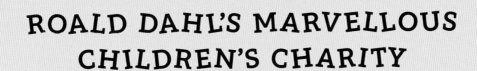

ROALD DAHL'S MARVELLOUS CHILDREN'S CHARITY

Roald Dahl's Marvellous Children's Charity provides much-needed specialist nurses and support for seriously ill children. The charity supports children and young people affected by complex, lifelong illnesses, including epilepsy, rare diseases, sickle cell anemia, and neuromuscular conditions.

Roald Dahl Nurse Specialists currently care for over twenty-four thousand seriously ill children across the UK. They are a vital lifeline to the children and their families. We believe every seriously ill child deserves a Roald Dahl Specialist Nurse.

Many marvelous people continue to do incredible work to support children, for the Marvellous Charity and beyond. We want to take this opportunity to celebrate some of these people. Please turn the page to discover a few of our **Marvellous Heroes!**

Marvelous
SIR QUENTIN BLAKE
is our hero!

Sir Quentin wields magic with his pens
and pencils and brings our favorite
children's book characters to life.
He is a phenomenally talented artist—
a legend of illustration—and his work
makes children all over the
world laugh and smile.

Marvelous
DAME JOANNA LUMLEY
is our hero!

Dame Joanna is a glorious actor and comedian.
She played the evil Aunt Spiker in the film of
James and the Giant Peach. But she is actually
one of the kindest and most generous people
we know. She is tireless in her support for
Roald Dahl's Marvellous Children's Charity
and so many other wonderful causes.

Marvelous
MARCUS RASHFORD
is our hero!

Marcus is of course a superstar on the soccer field, but also a superstar in campaigning to end child food poverty. Many children across the UK owe him thanks for making sure they don't go hungry.

Marvelous
GISELLE PADMORE-PAYNE
is our hero!

Giselle is an award-winning Roald Dahl Pediatric Nurse. She works tirelessly to care for and comfort children in the hospital. If we are ever sick, we can only hope that a nurse as wonderful as Giselle will care for us.

Hurrah for all our heroes!

BEFORE YOU START MAKING AND COOKING . . .

The recipes in this book are truly marvelous, and we hope you enjoy trying as many as you can.

It is really important that you have a responsible adult to help you for each one. We have added a note for steps in some of the recipes where it is absolutely essential that you have adult supervision (for instance, when dealing with an oven or hot pan, or chopping or blending food), but for each recipe we strongly advise that an adult is a key ingredient and that they are on hand at all times.

Some of the recipes are a little more challenging than others, and some will even teach you cooking skills you never knew about! In order to guide you through the trickier recipes, we have included hints and tips at the back of this book to help you be a champion chef. These include . . .

- A list of items and ingredients you'll need for the recipes, which can be found on **pages 92–101.**

- A guide for how to use cooking equipment, which can be found on **pages 102–107**.

- A list of cooking techniques and terms, which can be found on **pages 108–119.**

Finally, where you see this symbol **V** , it means the recipe is suitable for vegetarians. Where you see this symbol **Ve** , the recipe is suitable for vegans.

Happy cooking!

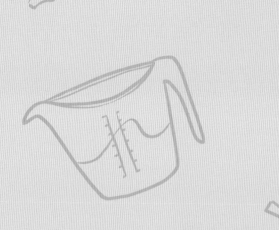

THE RECIPES!

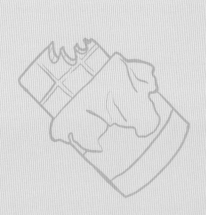

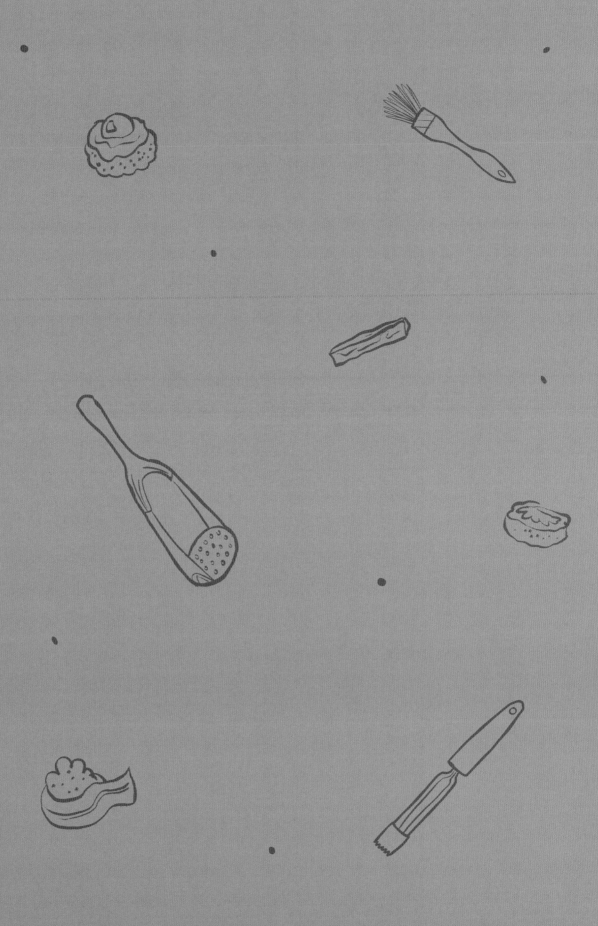

SMALL BITES
AND
STARTERS

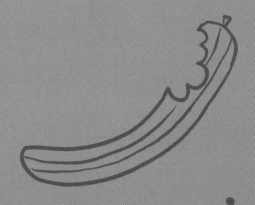

BULL'S EYES

FROM BOY

ILLUSTRATED BY RIKIN PAREKH

Keep an eye on these eyes—they disappear fast once made!

MAKES 8

YOU WILL NEED

EQUIPMENT

- fork

INGREDIENTS

- 3½ oz. rindless goat cheese (available in most supermarkets)
- 3½ tbsp. cream cheese
- 3 tbsp. sun-dried tomatoes, finely chopped
- 4 tbsp. black sesame seeds
- 1 large pickle
- 4 black olives, not pitted (the pit still inside)

WHAT YOU NEED TO DO

1 With the fork, mix the goat cheese, cream cheese, and sun-dried tomatoes until well mixed.

2 Roll the goat cheese mix into eight balls.

3 Put the black sesame seeds in a small bowl and roll the balls into the seeds one at a time, until the balls are completely covered.

4 Slice the pickle into eight thin slices and place one on top of each ball.

5 Slice the ends off the black olives—you need eight slices. Place one slice on top of each ball to finish.

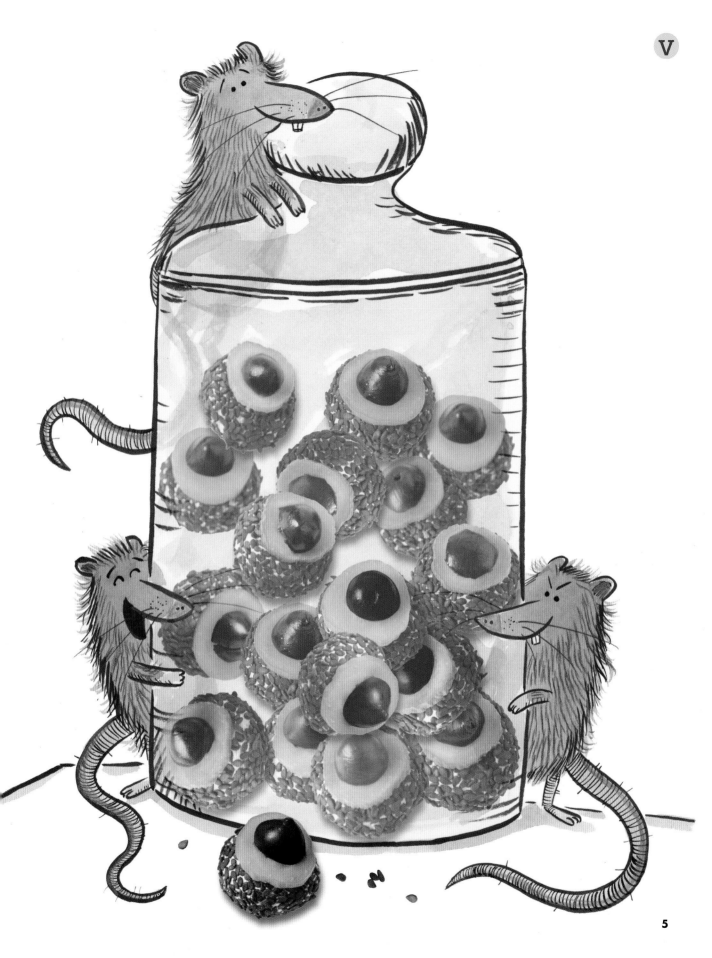

Dragon's FLESH

FROM JAMES AND THE GIANT PEACH

ILLUSTRATED BY TIM STEVENS

Here's what to do with freshly slayed dragon!

MAKES 4

YOU WILL NEED

EQUIPMENT

- baking tray lined with baking paper
- slotted spoon
- large bowl filled with cold water
- clean, dry tea towel
- blender or small food processor
- 4 wooden skewers

INGREDIENTS

- 1 8-oz. pack of Halloumi
- 16 small potatoes, each one around the same size
- 1 tbsp. olive oil for the potatoes
- 4 tbsp. fresh chives
- 4 tbsp. fresh basil
- 4 tbsp. extra-virgin olive oil for the herb oil
- pinch of salt
- 24 mint leaves
- 1 tbsp. nigella seeds (optional)

WHAT YOU NEED TO DO

1 Preheat the oven to 180°C/350°F/gas mark 4.

2 Cut the Halloumi into six triangles and then cut each piece through the middle (not to make it into a smaller triangle, but to halve the thickness). Now you need to "score" the Halloumi. This means cutting crisscross stripes into the Halloumi—but be very careful not to go all the way through. (If you do, don't panic! Your dragon's flesh will still taste delicious.)

3 Score the potatoes in the same way, but with the lines going in just one direction.

4 Rub the potatoes all over with ½ tbsp. of olive oil. Place cut side up on the baking tray and put into the preheated oven for 30 minutes, or until crispy.

5 Make sure you ask an adult to help with this next bit. While your potatoes are cooking, blanch the chives and basil in boiling water. This means you need to dip them into the water for about 30 seconds or just until they turn a bright green. Immediately lift them out using a slotted spoon and drop them into a bowl of very cold water.

6 Strain the now-cold herbs and carefully squeeze out all the liquid in a dry tea towel. Put into the blender (or small food processor) with 4 tbsp. of extra-virgin olive oil and a pinch of salt and process until completely smooth, but make sure it doesn't get warm (touch the outside of the blender to check the temperature). This will take 30–60 seconds, depending on what type of blender you're using. This will be your herb oil.

7 Next, brush the Halloumi slices with ½ tbsp. of olive oil and put into the oven, cut side up. Let them cook for 10–15 minutes, until they are crispy and golden. They should be ready at the same time as the potatoes. Carefully remove the potatoes and Halloumi from the oven and take them off the tray. Cool for a couple of minutes on a plate.

8 Take your skewers and start adding the potatoes and Halloumi slices, with a mint leaf in between. Add four potatoes and three pieces of Halloumi per skewer.

9 Drizzle generously with the herb oil, sprinkle with nigella seeds (if using), and eat!

GUMTWIZZLERS

FROM THE GIRAFFE AND THE PELLY AND ME

ILLUSTRATED BY DIANE EWEN

MAKES 10

YOU WILL NEED

EQUIPMENT

- roasting pan
- rolling pin
- baking tray lined with baking paper
- pastry brush

INGREDIENTS

- 1 medium-sized carrot, chopped into small cubes
- ½ zucchini, chopped into very small cubes
- salt and pepper
- 1 bunch of spring onions, finely chopped
- 1 pack of ready-rolled puff pastry (ideally all-butter)
- ½ cup grated cheddar cheese
- 1 egg yolk mixed with 1 tsp. milk

WHAT YOU NEED TO DO

1   Preheat the oven to 180°C/350°F/gas mark 4.

2   Put the carrot and zucchini in the roasting pan. Season with salt and pepper, and roast in the oven for 10 minutes. Add the spring onions 2 minutes before the end.

3   Remove the pan from the oven (careful—it will be hot!) and place the vegetables onto a plate to cool.

4   Unroll the puff pastry so it sits horizontally on the work surface. Once the vegetables are cool, lay them evenly on one half of the pastry, leaving a ½-in. gap around the edge. Sprinkle with the cheese and season with salt and pepper.

5   Fold the other half over and, with your rolling pin, lightly roll the edges of the pastry where they join, until the two halves are stuck together.

6   Chill the pastry in the fridge for 10 minutes, then cut into ¾-in.-wide strips (you should end up with ten strips in total).

7   Carefully pick up each strip of pastry from the middle. Using two hands, twist the pastry in opposite directions all the way to the edge to make a twisted roll. Place the rolls on your baking tray about 1 in. apart.

8   Chill in the fridge for 10 minutes. Next, brush the rolls with the egg-yolk-and-milk mixture. Do this very lightly—you don't want to cover them with too much.

9   Place in the oven for 20 minutes or until golden brown. When they're ready to eat, each Gumtwizzler should feel light and firm when you pick it up.

SNOZZCUMBERS

FROM THE **BFG**

ILLUSTRATED BY QUENTIN BLAKE

MAKES 4

YOU WILL NEED

EQUIPMENT

- vegetable peeler
- apple corer
- clean pastry brush

INGREDIENTS

- 2 large cucumbers
- 3½ oz. canned tuna
- 2 tomatoes, deseeded and chopped
- 3 cocktail pickles, finely chopped
- 3 tbsp. mayonnaise
- 3 tsp. poppy seeds
- salt and pepper

For the coating

- a little extra mayonnaise
- savory popcorn
- extra poppy seeds

WHAT YOU NEED TO DO

1 Peel the cucumbers and cut each one in half, then, with the point of the vegetable peeler, cut grooves along the length of each half.

2 Use the pointed end of the vegetable peeler to very carefully scoop little pits into the cucumber at random.

3 Cut off about 1½ in. from each half of the cucumber.

4 Hollow out the seeds from the body of each cucumber using the apple corer. Approach from both ends, but keep 2 in. of the center seed core to act as a plug later.

5 Stand each half in a tall glass and allow the excess liquids to drain (this will take about 30 minutes).

6 Thoroughly drain the tuna, and mix it with the chopped tomatoes, pickles, mayonnaise, and poppy seeds. Season with salt and pepper.

7 Use a teaspoon to fill the cucumbers with the tuna mixture, and pack it down with the teaspoon handle.

8 Replace ends, securing with previously made plugs.

9 Paint a little mayonnaise in the grooves on the outsides of the cucumber and carefully cover with poppy seeds using a teaspoon. (A steady hand is useful!)

10 Place a small piece of popcorn in each pit, putting a little mayonnaise in first to secure the popcorn. These can also be coated in poppy seeds if wished.

Sophie said the original Snozzcumber tasted of frog skin and rotten fish. The BFG said it tasted like cockroaches and slime-wanglers. What do you think?

DANDYPRATS

FROM JAMES AND THE GIANT PEACH

ILLUSTRATED BY TIM STEVENS

MAKES 4

YOU WILL NEED

EQUIPMENT

- muffin tin
- foil, lightly greased
- cocktail sticks
- 2 medium saucepans
- colander
- frying pan
- baking tray

INGREDIENTS

- 12 slices of streaky bacon (4 of them cut in half)
- 1¾ oz. uncooked macaroni
- 2 pinches of salt
- 2 tsp. olive oil
- 2¾ tbsp. double cream or heavy whipping cream
- 2¾ tbsp. full-fat milk
- ¼ cup cheddar cheese, grated
- pinch of nutmeg (optional)
- ¼ tsp. dijon mustard
- ½ tbsp. butter
- ¼ cup fresh bread crumbs
- ½ garlic clove, crushed or finely grated
- 1 tsp. fresh thyme, chopped (or use dried)

WHAT YOU NEED TO DO

1 Preheat the oven to 200°C/400°F/gas mark 6.

2 Turn the muffin tin upside down and wrap four of the inverted holes with very lightly greased foil.

3 Place two of the bacon half slices over the top of the foil-covered inverted muffin holes and two full bacon slices so they are wrapped around the bottoms. Secure any loose bits of bacon with cocktail sticks. Bake in the oven for 10 minutes.

4 Cook the macaroni in lightly salted boiling water according to the package instructions. Drain, add 1 tsp. of olive oil, toss to coat, and set aside.

5 When the bacon is crispy, remove from the oven and allow to cool. Then carefully remove each bacon cup from the bottom of the pan, remove any cocktail sticks, and place to one side on a paper towel.

6 Heat the cream and milk in a saucepan until almost boiling and then take off the heat. Stir in the cheddar, salt, nutmeg, and mustard until all the cheese is completely melted and the mix has thickened slightly.

7 Pour enough of the mix over the cooked macaroni until generously coated, and set aside.

8 Now heat the rest of the oil and the butter together in a frying pan, and, when completely melted, add the bread crumbs and fry over medium heat until they turn a golden color. Add the thyme and garlic when the bread crumbs are nearly cooked. When cooked, rest the mixture on a paper towel.

9 Now spoon the macaroni into the bacon cups and put back in the oven, on a baking tray, for 5 minutes.

10 When ready, remove from the oven and sprinkle a generous amount of the bread-crumb mix over the top to make them nice and crunchy. Then eat and enjoy!

DANDYCATS in **DANDYHATS** eating **DANDYPRATS**

HAS BEANS

FROM CHARLIE AND THE CHOCOLATE FACTORY

ILLUSTRATED BY IAN BECK

MAKES 6

YOU WILL NEED

EQUIPMENT

- saucepan with a lid
- medium-sized cookie cutter—the same size as or smaller than the muffin tin's holes
- muffin tin

INGREDIENTS

- 2 tbsp. vegetable oil
- 1 onion, finely chopped
- 2 garlic cloves, crushed
- 14-oz. can of chopped tomatoes
- 1 tbsp. tomato purée
- salt and pepper
- 2 soft flour tortillas
- 14-oz. can of navy beans, rinsed
- 2 tbsp. parmesan cheese, grated

WHAT YOU NEED TO DO

1 Preheat the oven to 160°C/325°F/gas mark 3.

2 Add the onion and a pinch of salt to the saucepan with oil. Cook over low heat with a lid on until the onions are very soft but haven't changed color—this could take up to 10 minutes. Add the garlic for the last 2 minutes.

3 When the onions are done, add the can of tomatoes, the tomato purée, and a pinch of salt and pepper. Cover the saucepan with a lid and continue cooking on a very low heat for 15 minutes.

4 While the filling is cooking, make the tortilla cups. Use your cookie cutter to cut three circles out of each of the tortillas.

5 Place the tortilla circles into the muffin tin. It's important to try and get the bottoms of them flat. Put them in the oven for 5 minutes until they have gone crispy, and then remove from the oven and allow to cool.

6 Add the beans to the tomato sauce and cook, still on a very low heat, for another 15 minutes.

7 When it is ready, carefully spoon the bean and tomato mix into the tortilla cups. Sprinkle with the parmesan and eat when cool enough!

GOBWANGLES

FROM THE GIRAFFE AND THE PELLY AND ME

ILLUSTRATED BY CHRIS WORMELL

MAKES 6

YOU WILL NEED

EQUIPMENT

- 2 saucepans—1 small, 1 medium (with lid)
- slotted spoon
- colander
- potato masher
- baking tray lined with baking paper
- heat-resistant bowl

INGREDIENTS

- 5 tbsp. butter
- half a medium-sized onion, finely chopped
- 2 large potatoes, peeled and chopped into large chunks
- pinch of salt
- 1 pack of ready-made filo pastry
- za'atar—a delicious Middle Eastern spice mix (use cumin seeds if you can't find any za'atar)

WHAT YOU NEED TO DO

1 Preheat the oven to 180°C/350°F/gas mark 4.

2 Fry the onion in a small saucepan in 3 tbsp. of butter, on the lowest heat possible. Do this until the onion is very soft but hasn't changed color.

3 Put the potatoes into a saucepan of cold water on high heat and bring to a boil with the lid on. After 10 minutes, lift one piece out carefully with a slotted spoon and pierce it with a knife. If the knife goes in easily, with no resistance, it's ready! If not, let the potatoes boil for another couple of minutes.

4 When the potatoes are ready, drain in a colander and then put back into the saucepan. Mash really well with your potato masher, along with the onion and the butter it was cooked in. Add a pinch of salt.

5 Unroll the filo pastry and cut the block into 30 squares, 3 × 3 in. each.

6 Melt the remaining 2 tbsp. of butter in a heat-resistant bowl in the microwave, or in a small saucepan on a gentle heat.

7 Now lay six square sheets of the filo pastry in a row a little less than 1 in. apart. Brush each one with the melted butter. Then put another sheet on top of each at a 45-degree angle and brush each one of those with butter. Then put a third sheet on top of each one at a 90-degree angle and brush each one of those with butter. Put two more sheets on top of each one at a 45-degree angle, one at a time, brushing each one with butter. You should end up with five layers of filo arranged like a star.

8 Put about a tablespoon of the mashed potato in the middle of each filo pile and, using a knife, lift the edges of the filo (it will tear if you try and use your hands). Gently squeeze the filo around the potato and then sprinkle with the za'atar.

9 Lay the Gobwangles on the baking tray and cook in the preheated oven for 20 minutes, or until the pastry is golden.

EARWIGS
Cooked in Slime

FROM **JAMES** AND THE **GIANT PEACH**

ILLUSTRATED BY EMILY WOODARD

MAKES 6

YOU WILL NEED

EQUIPMENT

- baking tray lined with baking paper
- saucepan
- sieve or colander
- clean, damp tea towel
- cutting board

INGREDIENTS

- 6 raw prawns
- 2 tbsp. coconut milk
- 1 garlic clove, finely chopped
- pinch of salt
- 1 oz. rice noodles
- 6 rice paper rolls (or spring roll wrappers)
- 12 mint leaves
- ¾ oz. red cabbage, finely sliced
- ¾ oz. carrot, cut into very thin matchsticks

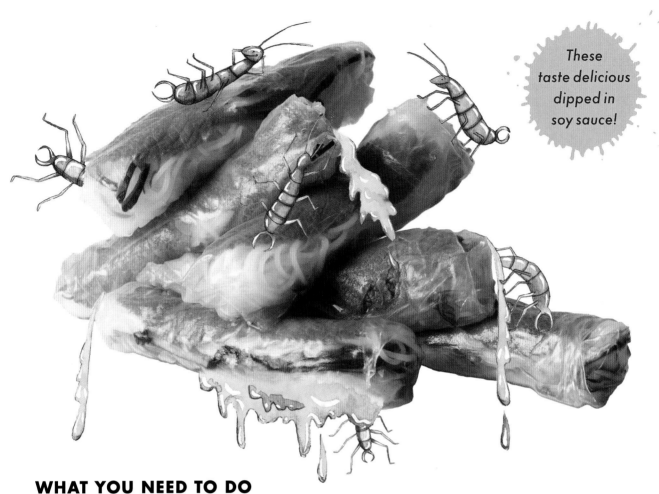

These taste delicious dipped in soy sauce!

WHAT YOU NEED TO DO

1. Preheat the oven to 150°C/300°F/gas mark 2.

2. Peel the prawns, and clean thoroughly using tap water. Then slice in half lengthways. (If there is a dark vein down the back of the prawn, remove it!) Place in a bowl.

3. Spoon the coconut milk and garlic over the prawns and mix well so that they're completely covered. Place the prawns on a baking tray, sprinkle with a pinch of salt, and put in the oven for 5 minutes.

4. As the prawns cook, they curl up, a bit like earwigs! Remove them from the oven, place on a plate, and allow to cool.

5. Cook the rice noodles in a pan of boiling water for 2 minutes. Ask an adult to help you drain it in a sieve or colander and rinse under cold water until completely cool.

6. Next, get a bowl of cold water and put one sheet of rice paper into it for a minute or until it's soft. Then carefully take the rice paper out of the water. Be extra careful as you do this, because the paper can rip easily.

7. Spread the rice paper on the tea towel, which should be spread over the cutting board. Place two mint leaves down the middle, then place a teaspoonful of cabbage on top, then a teaspoon of carrot. (You'll need enough cabbage and carrot for five more of these, so use sparingly!) Add two prawn halves and a small bit of the rice noodles.

8. Now roll it up. To do this, fold the bottom half of the paper up and then fold each side over. Then roll it up from the bottom.

9. Repeat with the other sheets of rice paper, and your earwigs in slime are ready to eat!

GUMGLOTTERS

FROM THE GIRAFFE AND THE PELLY AND ME

ILLUSTRATED BY JOEL STEWART

You can remove the bacon to make this dish vegetarian!

MAKES 12

YOU WILL NEED

EQUIPMENT

- small saucepan
- whisk
- wooden spoon
- baking tray lined with plastic wrap
- deep, wide saucepan
- digital thermometer (optional)
- tongs
- paper towels

INGREDIENTS

For the fries

- 4 cups water
- 7 oz. polenta (not the precooked kind—available in most supermarkets)
- 2½ tbsp. parmesan, grated
- 1½ tbsp. butter
- 1 oz. bacon, cooked and finely chopped
- 2 tsp. rosemary, finely chopped
- ½ cup peas, cooked and mashed
- salt and pepper
- ¾ cup flour
- 2 cups vegetable oil, or enough to fill the pan to 2 or 2½ in. deep

For the dip

- 1 cup mayonnaise
- 2 roasted red peppers (from a jar is fine), very finely chopped
- 1 garlic clove, very finely chopped
- salt and pepper

WHAT YOU NEED TO DO

1 Boil the water in a small saucepan and then slowly whisk in the polenta. Keep whisking until there are no lumps left, and then switch to a wooden spoon. Be careful—this gets very hot!

2 When the mixture is stiff enough for a wooden spoon to stand upright without you holding it, add in the parmesan, butter, bacon, rosemary, peas, salt, and pepper. Taste, then add more salt and pepper if necessary.

3 Spread the mix onto the plastic-wrap-lined baking tray in a rectangular shape, approximately 8 × 3 in. Cover with more plastic wrap and chill in the fridge for 30 minutes.

4 While it's chilling, mix all the dip ingredients together.

5 When the polenta mix is cold, cut into roughly 12 fries and toss gently in flour so that they are completely covered. Shake off any excess flour.

6 Ask an adult to heat the oil in the saucepan to 180°C/350°F (or hot enough so a fry bubbles as it's added to the oil).

7 Add a few fries at a time to the deep saucepan, and turn them using kitchen tongs occasionally as they fry. When they are golden brown on all sides—this will take about 6 minutes—remove from the oil and drain on a paper towel.

8 Try to cook them all before starting to eat—though this might be difficult! Serve alongside the dip.

MINCED DOODLEBUGS

FROM JAMES AND THE GIANT PEACH

ILLUSTRATED BY ABE ODEDINA

MAKES 16–18

YOU WILL NEED

EQUIPMENT

- small saucepan
- mixing bowl

INGREDIENTS

- 7 oz. broccoli florets
- pinch of salt
- 2 eggs, beaten
- 1 cup cheddar cheese, grated
- 1 oz. oats
- ½ tsp. ground cumin
- 1 tsp. dried oregano
- 1 tsp. crushed or finely grated garlic
- 2 spring onions, finely chopped
- ½ cup dried bread crumbs
- 1 tbsp. black sesame seeds
- 1 tbsp. white sesame seeds

For the dip

- ½ cup yogurt
- 1 tbsp. chopped mint
- juice from ½ lemon

WHAT YOU NEED TO DO

1 Preheat the oven to 180°C/350°F/gas mark 4.

2 Cook the broccoli in lightly salted boiling water until bright green (this will only take a couple of minutes). Then chop each piece of broccoli up into small chunks.

3 Mix the beaten eggs, cheddar, broccoli, oats, cumin, oregano, garlic, bread crumbs, and spring onions in a bowl.

4 Shape the mixture into what you think a doodlebug would look like.

5 Sprinkle with the sesame seeds.

6 Bake for 10–15 minutes, until they look lightly browned.

7 While your doodlebugs are cooking, mix all of the remaining ingredients together to make the dip.

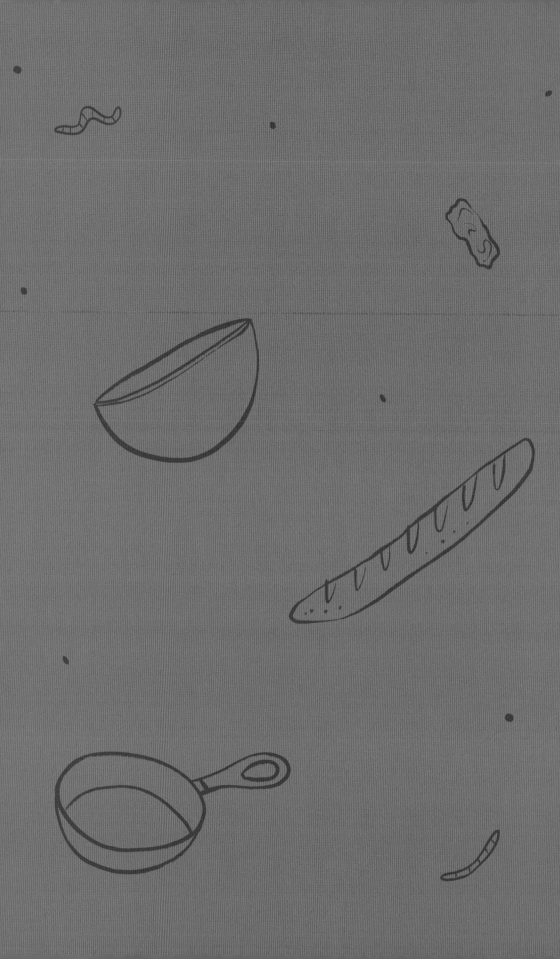

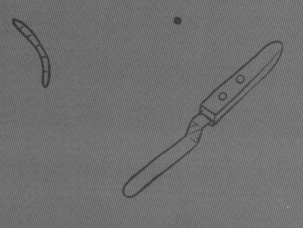

MAIN MEALS
AND
CENTERPIECES

HOT DOGS

FROM **JAMES** AND THE **GIANT PEACH**

ILLUSTRATED BY QUENTIN BLAKE

MAKES 8

YOU WILL NEED

EQUIPMENT

- weighing scales
- rolling pin
- roasting pan
- pastry brush

INGREDIENTS

- 17½ oz. packet of bread-dough mix
- 8 sausages (these could be vegetarian sausages)
- 8 strips of back bacon (optional)
- tomato ketchup
- mustard (your favorite kind)
- 1 egg yolk

WHAT YOU NEED TO DO

1 Preheat the oven to 200°C/400°F/gas mark 6.

2 Follow instructions on the bread-mix packet to make the dough.

3 While the dough is rising, cook the sausages in the oven. If you are using the bacon, wrap it around the sausages before cooking. When they are light brown (after about 15 minutes), take them out and allow to cool.

4 When the dough has doubled in size, split it into 8 pieces (weighing approximately 2½ oz. each).

5 Roll each piece of dough into a circle roughly 5 in. across.

6 Place a sausage in the middle of one of the dough circles and spread it with a small amount of ketchup and/or mustard.

7 Carefully roll it up (keeping it quite tight), and fold in the ends so that the entire sausage is covered.

8 Do the same with the rest of the sausages until you have eight portions. Place in the roasting pan.

9 Brush with the egg yolk and allow to rise again.

10 When they have doubled in size again (after 20–30 minutes), place back in the preheated oven and cook for 20–25 minutes or until golden.

11 Allow to cool for 5 minutes before eating.

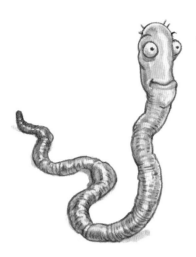

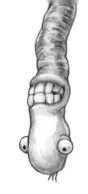

WORMY
Spaghetti
FROM THE TWITS

ILLUSTRATED BY TIM STEVENS

SERVES 4–5

YOU WILL NEED

EQUIPMENT

- 2 large saucepans
- food processor or stick blender

INGREDIENTS

For the sauce

- 2 tbsp. sunflower oil
- 1 onion, roughly chopped
- 2 celery sticks, chopped (optional)
- 1 garlic clove, crushed
- 14-oz. can of plum tomatoes
- 1 tbsp. tomato purée
- 1 tbsp. parsley, chopped
- 1 bay leaf
- 1 tsp. sugar
- salt and pepper
- 2 carrots, grated

For the pasta

- pinch of salt
- 50 g fusilli col buco spaghetti (curly spaghetti, but you can use regular spaghetti if this isn't available)
- 225 g tricolor spaghetti (spinach, whole-wheat, and plain)
- 1½ cups cheddar cheese, grated

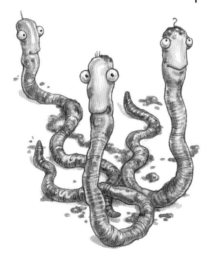

WHAT YOU NEED TO DO

1   Heat the oil in a saucepan and sweat the onion, celery (optional), and garlic until soft (for instructions on "sweating," see page 118).

2   Add the remaining ingredients for the sauce except the carrots, bring to a boil, and then reduce heat slightly and allow to simmer for 30 minutes.

3   Remove the bay leaf and blend or process the sauce until smooth.

4   Return the sauce to the saucepan, add salt and pepper to taste, and keep warm.

5   Meanwhile, bring a large saucepan of water to a boil. Then add the salt and both kinds of spaghetti. Cook until tender (stirring the pasta thoroughly so it doesn't stick together), and drain.

6   Reheat the sauce and fold in the carrot until it is warm.

7   Divide out the spaghetti onto serving plates, spoon over the sauce, and garnish with grated cheese.

This recipe can be made vegan if you don't include the cheddar cheese!

Serve with a tasty green salad!

HANSEL AND GRETEL
Spare Ribs

FROM **RHYME STEW**

ILLUSTRATED BY QUENTIN BLAKE

SERVES 4

YOU WILL NEED

EQUIPMENT

- medium-sized, deep roasting pan lined with baking paper
- large mixing bowl
- metal tongs

INGREDIENTS

- 24 oz. spare ribs
- 1 tbsp. Worcester sauce
- 1 tbsp. soy sauce
- 1 tbsp. English mustard
- 1 tbsp. tomato ketchup
- 1 tbsp. runny honey
- ½ tsp. fine salt
- ½ tsp. black pepper

WHAT YOU NEED TO DO

1 Preheat the oven to 200°C/400°F/gas mark 6.

2 Mix all the ingredients except the spare ribs together in a bowl—this is your marinade.

3 Add the spare ribs to the bowl and stir together with the tongs until the ribs are nicely coated in the marinade.

4 Put the ribs and the mixture into the roasting pan, then add 2 cups of water, which should cover the ribs completely. Space out the ribs so that they cook evenly.

5 Place the pan in the oven. You need to turn the ribs with the tongs every 20 minutes for about 1¼ to 1½ hours. If the sauce looks a bit dry during cooking, top up with another ⅓ to ½ cup of water and mix in well. The ribs should be well cooked and crunchy and the sauce sticky when ready to eat.

6 Remove the ribs from the oven and transfer to a serving dish. Let the ribs cool down for a few minutes before digging in!

THE ENORMOUS CROCODILE

FROM THE ENORMOUS CROCODILE

ILLUSTRATED BY QUENTIN BLAKE

MAKES 1 CENTERPIECE

YOU WILL NEED

EQUIPMENT

- wire coat hanger (thoroughly cleaned and with the hook cut off)
- frying pan
- palette knife
- cocktail sticks

If you wish to eat the croc straight away, either leave the coat hanger out or make sure you remove it before eating. His jaws will be closed, but he'll still be delicious! Warn your guests that there are sharp cocktail sticks in the crocodile's eyes and legs.

INGREDIENTS

For the crocodile body

- 1 large baguette (body)
- 3½ oz. whole blanched almonds (teeth)
- 14 oz. frozen chopped spinach (skin)
- 2 globe artichokes (scales and eye sockets)
- 1 slice of ham (tongue)
- 1 egg, hard-boiled (eyeballs)
- 1 black olive, cut in half (pupils)
- 2 cooked sausages (legs)
- 12 cocktail pickles (toes)

For the egg filling

(quantities depend on the size of the baguette)

- 6–8 eggs, hard-boiled
- salt and pepper

- 3–4 tbsp. mayonnaise
- 1 carton of watercress

WHAT YOU NEED TO DO

1 Slice one end of the baguette horizontally in half along one-third of its length. This is the crocodile's mouth.

2 Now slice the other end horizontally to make the crocodile's body, leaving ½ to ¾ in. unsliced to make his neck. Carefully lift off the top of his body section.

3 Hollow out the top and bottom of his body. Then hollow out the lower jaw, leaving a wide border.

4 Insert his almond teeth into the border. Secure any loose teeth with mayonnaise.

5 Fold the coat hanger in half and carefully place it inside his mouth to give the jaws support.

6 Defrost the spinach and cook in a frying pan for 5 minutes. Then squeeze out all the moisture from the spinach. Set aside to cool.

7 Boil the artichokes for 30–40 minutes, drain, and set aside. When cold, pluck off the leaves, discard the hairy chokes, and keep the hearts (a treat for adults later).

8 For the filling, season and chop the hard-boiled eggs. Mix in with the mayonnaise and watercress.

9 Stuff the crocodile's body with the egg filling. Put in his tongue (the ham) over the top of the filling in his mouth.

10 Spread the cooked spinach over the body with a small palette knife. Mold the mixture to look like scaly skin. Position the artichoke leaves to look like the scales on the crocodile's body.

11 Next, to make the eyes, cut the hard-boiled egg in half and turn the egg yolks around so that they protrude. Add the olive halves to be the crocodile's pupils, and secure to the face with cocktail sticks.

12 For the legs, slice the sausages in half and position. Hold in place with cocktail sticks.

13 For the toes, add the cocktail pickles.

MAGIC MIXED DREAM

FROM THE
BFG

ILLUSTRATED BY ALEXIS DEACON

MAKES 1 LARGE BOWL

YOU WILL NEED

EQUIPMENT

- large roasting pan lined with baking paper
- frying pan
- plastic wrap
- small saucepan
- blender
- 3 jam jars
- large bowl

INGREDIENTS

- 9 bell peppers (3 each of red, orange, and yellow)
- 2 garlic cloves
- ¾–1 in. fresh ginger, peeled and grated
- 1 tbsp. olive oil
- 2½ cups chicken or vegetable stock

WHAT YOU NEED TO DO

1 Preheat the oven to 200°C/400°F/gas mark 6.

2 Cut the tops off of all 9 peppers. Remove the seeds and white pith from the middle of each pepper and cut each one in half.

3 Place the pepper halves cut side down in your roasting pan, and put in the preheated oven for 30 minutes, or until the skin on the peppers is blistered and black in parts.

4 While the peppers are roasting, gently fry the garlic and ginger in a frying pan, in the oil, over low heat. When they turn golden brown, turn off the heat.

5 When the peppers are cooked, remove from the oven and cover with plastic wrap. Leave them to steam for about 5 minutes.

6 Remove the plastic (be careful because the tray and peppers might still be hot). Remove as much of the pepper skin as possible, and keep all the liquid that's left at the bottom of the pan.

7 Heat the stock to a gentle simmer, then put one-third of the stock, one-third of the pepper liquid, and the yellow peppers only into the blender. Blend until completely smooth and then pour into one of the jam jars. Do exactly the same with the orange and red peppers.

8 Now comes the dream mixing. Pour an equal amount of each color into the bowl. Do the yellow first and then the orange and red at the same time immediately after. You should now have three separate colors in the bowl.

9 Give the mixture a swirl. You have now mixed the dream and you're ready for the magic—eating it all up!

HOT NOODLES MADE FROM POODLES

on a Slice of Garden Hose

FROM **JAMES** AND THE **GIANT PEACH**

ILLUSTRATED BY QUENTIN BLAKE

SERVES 2–3

YOU WILL NEED

EQUIPMENT

- large saucepan
- large bowl filled with cold water
- slotted spoon
- paper towels
- food processor
- plastic wrap
- rolling pin
- colander
- 2 coat hangers (thoroughly cleaned)

INGREDIENTS

- ¾ cup flat-leaf parsley
- 2 large eggs
- 1⅔ cups plain flour
- salt and pepper
- 1 tbsp. olive oil
- 1 tbsp. parmesan cheese, grated

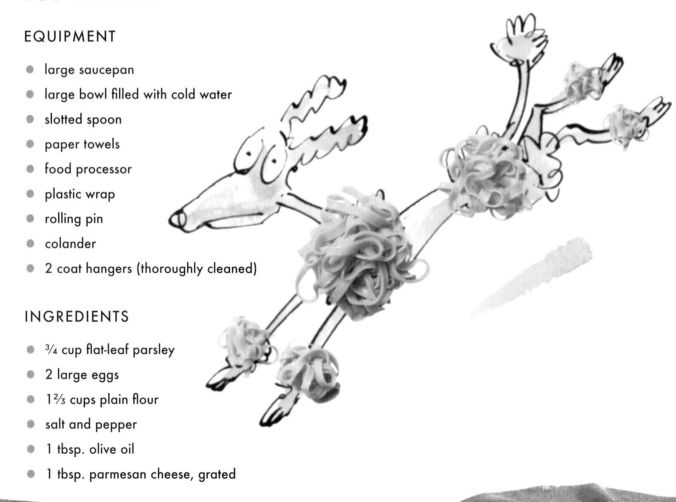

WHAT YOU NEED TO DO

1   Bring a saucepan of water to a boil and place the large bowl of cold water as close as possible to it. When the water is boiling, drop the parsley into it—count to 5 and then take it out with a slotted spoon and drop it straight into the bowl of very cold water.

2   Squeeze the parsley very hard—you want to get all the water out—and then place it on a paper towel and set aside.

3   Put the eggs and flour into the processor and process for 2 minutes. You should have a soft but not sticky dough.

4   Take out of the food processor and knead on a lightly floured surface for 2 minutes. Cover with plastic wrap and let it rest for 15 minutes.

5   After 15 minutes, place about one-quarter of the dough in the food processor with the parsley, and blend until the parsley is completely mixed in and the dough has turned garden-hose green. Take out and place on a floured surface. Using the rolling pin, roll it out as thinly as possible, and then cut it into 1½-in.-wide strips to make your flattened garden hose.

6   Hang the strips over a coat hanger to dry out while you make the poodle noodles.

7   Roll out the poodle (the other batch of dough) as thinly as possible. Then roll it up like a swiss roll and slice it very thinly.

8   Unravel these slices and hang on a coat hanger too. Allow to dry for 30 minutes.

9   Bring the saucepan of water back to a boil and add 2 tsp. of salt, then put the pieces of garden hose in and cook at a rapid boil for 3–5 minutes.

10   Take out with a slotted spoon and drain in a colander.

11   Put the noodles in the boiling water and cook for 2–5 minutes depending on the thickness of the dough. Drain using the colander with the garden hose in, and then put everything back into the saucepan with the heat turned off. Toss in the olive oil and some salt and pepper to taste.

12   Lay the garden hose on a plate and top with the noodles and parmesan.

MR. TWIT'S
Beard Food
FROM THE TWITS

ILLUSTRATED BY QUENTIN BLAKE

SERVES 4

YOU WILL NEED

EQUIPMENT

- saucepan
- potato masher
- baking tray lined with baking paper

INGREDIENTS

- 2 large potatoes
- knob of butter
- 3½ tbsp. milk
- ⅓ cup frozen peas
- 1 medium mushroom or ¼ tomato (nose)
- 1 egg, hard-boiled (eyes)
- 1 olive, cut in half (pupils)
- 1 slice of bread, toasted (eyebrows)
- 1 small mushroom cap, cut in half (ears)
- 8 cocktail sausages
- 6 small pieces of rolled-up bread or pine nuts (teeth)
- shoestring potato chips (bristles and hair)
- pretzel sticks (bristles)
- 6 oz. baked beans
- tomato ketchup
- a little grated cheese
- gravy (optional)

WHAT YOU NEED TO DO

1 Peel the potatoes and cook in boiling water until soft. Drain and mash with the butter and milk.

2 Cook the peas according to package instructions. Grill the mushroom, or, if you are using a tomato for his nose, remove the seeds and cut the flesh into a nose shape.

To assemble Mr. Twit's face

3 FACE: Draw an oval shape on the baking paper and turn over. With a little of the mashed potato, form a base for his face on the oval.

4 EYES: Peel the hard-boiled egg and cut in half. Remove the yolks and turn them upside down, so they form domes on the whites of the egg. Place on the plate for his eyes. Then add the half olives as pupils.

5 EYEBROWS: Cut his eyebrows from the toast. (It should be one continual strip as Mr. Twit's eyebrows join in the middle.)

6 NOSE: Vertically cut the grilled mushroom in half and place on the plate as his nose (cut edge up). Alternatively, use the prepared tomato from step 2.

7 EARS: Place half the small mushroom for each ear.

8 HAIR AND BEARD: With the remaining mashed potato, form a base for his hair and beard.

9 MOUTH: Cut 3 cocktail sausages in half and assemble to create lips with a gap in between. Cut 2 more sausages so they are still joined at one end—these will form the corners of his mouth.

10 TEETH: Use tiny pieces of bread rolled and pressed between your fingers into tooth shapes, and position in his mouth. Alternatively, use pine nuts.

11 BEARD: Build his beard out of the remaining shoestring potato chips (bristles) and remaining sausages (cut into little pieces), pretzel sticks, peas, baked beans, tomato ketchup, and anything else you want on the beard!

12 To warm up, place in the oven at 180°C/350°F/gas mark 4 for 10–15 minutes.

13 Sprinkle the grated cheese (and gravy, if you like!) over his beard.

MICE with RICE

FROM JAMES AND THE GIANT PEACH

ILLUSTRATED BY CHRIS RIDDELL

SERVES 4

YOU WILL NEED

EQUIPMENT

- baking tray or roasting pan lined with baking paper
- small/medium saucepan with a well-fitting lid
- sieve

INGREDIENTS

For the mice (the lamb)

- 7 oz. minced lamb or 4 mice (not really—you need the lamb)
- 1 medium onion, very finely chopped
- ½ tsp. salt
- 3 tsp. za'atar—if you can't find this in your supermarket, use dried mint
- 8 flaked almonds
- 12 black peppercorns
- 1 piece of whole-wheat spaghetti, cooked

For the rice

- ½ onion, finely chopped
- 1 tsp. butter
- 1 cup white basmati rice
- 1 garlic clove
- ½ tsp. turmeric
- 1½ cups cold water or chicken/vegetable stock
- ⅓ cup pistachios, chopped
- 1 tbsp. parsley, chopped
- ¼ tsp. salt

WHAT YOU NEED TO DO

FOR THE LAMB (THE MICE!)

1 Preheat the oven to 180°C/350°F/gas mark 4.

2 Mix together the minced lamb and onion in a bowl. Add the salt and za'atar. You need to mix this all together really well with both hands for at least 2 minutes.

3 Using wet hands, divide the mix into four equal balls.

4 Place onto a baking tray (or a roasting pan lined with baking paper) and set aside.

FOR THE RICE (AND TO FINISH OFF YOUR MICE)

1 Cook the onion in the butter on a very low heat, with the lid on, until soft but not colored.

2 Wash the rice in the sieve under cold running water until the draining water looks clear. Let it drain for a couple of minutes.

3 While it's draining, add the garlic and turmeric to the onion, stir well, and sauté for about a minute. Then add the rice and the cold water (or stock).

4 Put the lid on the saucepan and turn the heat up to full. It's very important not to take the lid off for the entire time that the rice is cooking. After a minute, you will see steam coming out of the rice; at this point, turn the heat to the lowest possible setting, and allow to cook for 10 minutes.

5 After the 10 minutes, take the rice off the heat and leave for 15 minutes (with the lid still on).

6 Cook the lamb mice in the oven for 15 minutes, then take out and allow to cool for 5 minutes.

7 While they are cooling, stir the pistachios and parsley into the rice, along with the salt.

8 Ask an adult to make little slits with a sharp knife where you're going to put the ears, eyes, and tails on the mice. Then put the almonds in for the ears, the black peppercorns for eyes, and the spaghetti (cut into four) to be the tails.

9 Arrange the rice in a big pile on a serving plate, and then carefully place the mice on top.

DOC SPENCER'S PIE

FROM **DANNY** THE **CHAMPION** OF THE **WORLD**

ILLUSTRATED BY QUENTIN BLAKE

MAKES 6

YOU WILL NEED

EQUIPMENT

- mixing bowl
- pastry brush
- baking tray

INGREDIENTS

- 4 slices of ham, chopped
- 4 hard-boiled eggs, chopped
- 1 tbsp. mayonnaise
- 2 tbsp. cheddar cheese, grated
- salt and pepper
- 1 pack ready-made filo pastry
- 3 tbsp. butter, melted
- 1 tbsp. sesame seeds

WHAT YOU NEED TO DO

1 Preheat the oven to 200°C/400°F/gas mark 6.

2 Mix together ham, eggs, mayonnaise, cheddar cheese, salt, and pepper.

3 Cut a sheet of filo pastry in half widthways. Lay one piece on top of the other.

4 Brush with melted butter. Put 2 tbsp. of the egg and ham mix onto the pastry and carefully roll into a cigar shape, folding in the sides so that it is safely sealed.

5 Brush the top with melted butter and sprinkle with sesame seeds. Continue until all the mixture is used up, or you lose interest (as the rest can be a delicious sandwich filling).

6 Bake in the preheated oven for 15–20 minutes or until golden brown.

7 Allow to cool for 10 minutes before you eat them—otherwise you'll burn your tongue!

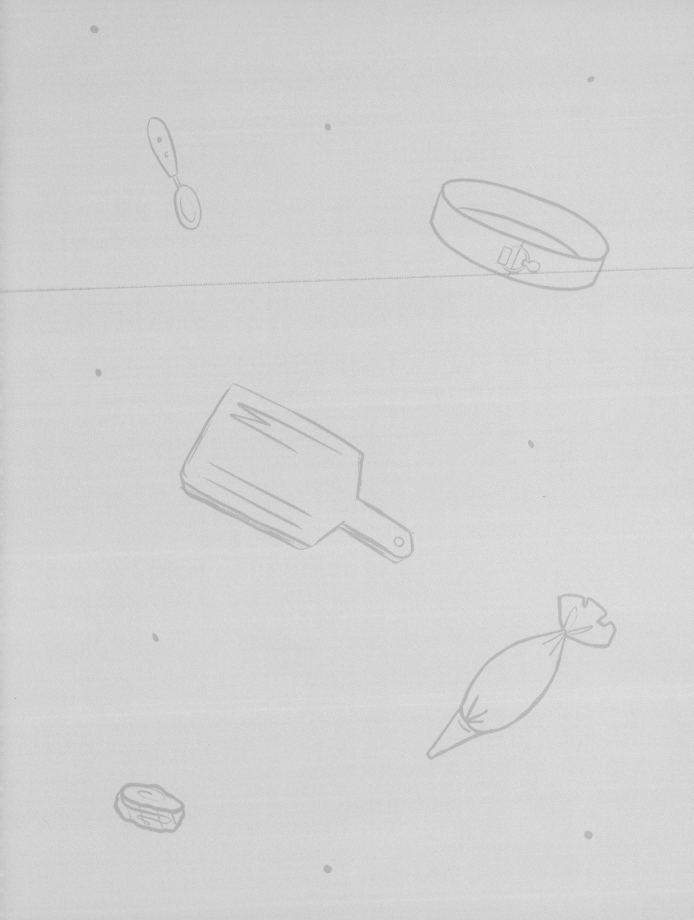

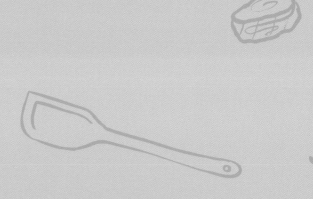

DESSERTS

MONKEY BARK

INSPIRED BY **THE TWITS**

ILLUSTRATED BY EMMA CHICHESTER CLARK

Serves four humans or two hungry monkeys.

MAKES 1 MONKEY BARK TRUNK AND 1 LOG

YOU WILL NEED

EQUIPMENT

- baking sheet
- black/brown felt-tip pen
- baking paper
- small round cookie cutter (1–2 in.)
- small saucepan
- 2 medium-sized heat-resistant bowls that will fit over the saucepan
- rolling pin
- cutting board
- pastry brush

INGREDIENTS

- ¼ tsp. soft butter
- 1 cup white chocolate
- 2 cookies of your choice (sandwich cookies or shortbread, for example)
- 2 tbsp. chopped nuts
- 1 tbsp. raisins, chopped (optional)
- 1 tbsp. mini marshmallows, chopped (optional)
- ¾ cup milk chocolate
- 1 tbsp. powdered sugar
- 1 tsp. cocoa powder
- 1 tsp. dried mint, crushed to a powder (you can crumble it up finely with your fingers)

WHAT YOU NEED TO DO

1 Using your imagination or a photo of a tree trunk, draw a tree-trunk shape onto the baking paper with a felt-tip pen. The trunk should be about 8 in. high and 2 in. wide, and the base about 4 or 5 in. wide. Lay the paper flat on your baking sheet (making sure the side you've drawn on is face down).

2 To make the log, grease the inside of the cookie cutter with the butter. Line the inside of the cutter smoothly with a strip of baking paper that measures ¼ in. more than the height of the cutter. Place it on the baking sheet to the side of your tree trunk. You are now ready to make your tree and log.

5 Add the crushed cookies, nuts, raisins, and marshmallows to the chocolate. Stir to combine. Lick the spoon to make sure it tastes good (it will!).

6 Using a tablespoon, spread most of the white chocolate mix onto your trunk template. Fill your cookie cutter with a few tablespoons of the mixture (aim for about 1–1½ in. high).

9 When the log of chocolate has set, push it through the cutter and out, then peel away the baking paper. Decorating time! Using a tablespoon, drizzle the thickened milk chocolate onto the trunk and spread to coat completely. It will start to set as it touches the cold wood, so work quickly!

10 Using a fork, make bark-type markings in the chocolate trunk before it sets. Use the pastry brush to paint some milk chocolate onto the sides of your log too. Then place everything back into the fridge to set for a few minutes.

3 Fill the saucepan with 1 in. of water and bring to a simmer on the lowest heat possible. Break up the white chocolate into one of the bowls and set the bowl over the saucepan. Let the chocolate slowly melt and stir it once or twice. (You can also use a microwave to melt the chocolate—see page 116 to find out how.)

4 Turn the heat off and let the chocolate finish melting. Meanwhile, crush the cookies into powdery crumbs with a rolling pin on a cutting board (ensure there are some larger pieces remaining).

7 Transfer the tray to the fridge and let everything set for about 30 minutes.

8 While you are waiting for the wood to set, start to make your bark. Melt the milk chocolate in the same way you did with the white. Take the bowl of milk chocolate off the heat to cool a little as it needs to be quite thick to make the bark.

11 There will be some melted chocolate left over, so use that to make a thin second layer of wood on the log and on the tree. Allow to chill for a few more minutes in the fridge.

12 With a clean, dry brush, decorate the set chocolate bark with the powdered sugar, cocoa powder, and dried mint. Sit back and admire your masterpiece, then dig in!

SWUDGE

FROM CHARLIE AND THE CHOCOLATE FACTORY

ILLUSTRATED BY CHRIS RIDDELL

Swudge is a soft, minty sugar that looks like grass.

MAKES 1

YOU WILL NEED

EQUIPMENT

- 4 × 8-in. cake pans
- foil
- electric hand mixer
- spatula
- large metal spoon

INGREDIENTS

- 4 egg whites
- pinch of salt
- 1¼ cups caster sugar
- ¼ tsp. mint extract
- ½ tsp. white wine vinegar
- 1 tsp. green food coloring
- ¾ cup pistachios, chopped
- 1 tbsp. green sugar/sprinkles (these might need to be purchased online)
- 3½ oz. raspberries
- 8 oz. mascarpone

WHAT YOU NEED TO DO

1   Preheat the oven to 180°C/350°F/gas mark 4.

2   Line the cake pans with the foil and lightly oil.

3   In a bowl, beat the egg whites with a pinch of salt until stiff and then gradually beat in the caster sugar a tablespoon at a time. Then beat in the mint extract, vinegar, and green food coloring until very stiff. Fold in the pistachios, very gently, with the metal spoon.

4   Divide the mix between the four cake pans and spread evenly with a spatula.

5   Sprinkle the green sugar or sprinkles on top of each one.

6   Place two pans on the oven's middle shelf and two on the shelf below. Bake for 20 minutes, then swap the pans around. Bake for a further 20 minutes, but if the mixture starts going slightly brown, turn the heat down, because you don't want to burn the cakes.

7   While the cakes are cooking, put the raspberries in a bowl and crush with a spoon or fork. Then add the mascarpone and mix thoroughly. Set aside.

8   When the cakes are cooked, let them cool in the pans. When each one is completely cool, lift it out of the pan and carefully remove the foil.

9   (Do this last bit only when you're ready to eat, otherwise it will go soggy!) You're now going to layer up the four layers of cake, so choose the best-looking one for the top! Put the bottom one on the plate you're going to serve on, and spread the mascarpone mix on top. Now put the next layer on top, and do the same to the top of this one. Repeat with the next two layers, and it's ready to eat!

SCARLET
Scorchdroppers
FROM THE GIRAFFE AND THE PELLY AND ME

ILLUSTRATED BY JOEL STEWART

MAKES 6

YOU WILL NEED

EQUIPMENT

- 6 very long wooden skewers
- 3 small bowls
- 3 disposable piping bags
- 3 glasses
- spatula

INGREDIENTS

- 42 strawberries (you can of course use fewer, but ideally a minimum of 36)
- ½ cup dark chocolate
- ½ cup milk chocolate
- ½ cup white chocolate
- edible glitter, sprinkles, luster powder, or edible gold and silver balls—or all four if you can find them!

WHAT YOU NEED TO DO

1 Rinse and hull the strawberries. (Hulling means you need to cut the green and white bits off the strawberries.)

2 Thread 7 strawberries onto each skewer.

3 Break the chocolate into small pieces, and place each type into one of the small bowls.

4 Fold your piping bags over the rims of the glasses so that each is opened up completely in the glass.

5 Now you're going to need to melt all the chocolate. You can do this either on the defrost setting in the microwave or by putting the bowls over a saucepan of simmering water (see page 116 for more information on melting chocolate).

6 When melted, scrape each type of chocolate into each of the three piping bags with a spatula. Twist the tops to close the piping bags and squeeze all the chocolate down to the bottom.

7 Make a very small hole in the bottom of each piping bag once you've removed it from the glass. Starting with the dark chocolate, drizzle the chocolate over the skewers by moving the bag very quickly from side to side. Then repeat with the milk chocolate, then the white chocolate. You need to do all the chocolates quite quickly so that they're not completely set before the next step.

8 Sprinkle the strawberries with edible glitter, sprinkles, luster powder, or gold and silver balls—or all four!

ISKREM

ILLUSTRATED BY LAUREN O'HARA

MAKES 8–10 ICE CREAM BARS

YOU WILL NEED

EQUIPMENT

- large mixing bowl
- whisk or electric hand mixer
- ice cream (or ice pop) molds with sticks
- patience (because the Iskrem has to freeze overnight!)

INGREDIENTS

- 2½ cups double cream
- 14 oz. condensed milk
- 2 tsp. vanilla extract
- 14 oz. caramel condensed milk
- 4 tbsp. freeze-dried raspberries, crushed (leave these in the freezer for now)
- 2 tbsp. toasted hazelnuts, chopped (see page 114 for how to toast nuts!)

This means ice cream in Norwegian. Roald Dahl's parents were from Norway, and the country had a big influence on his books.

Here is a very special version of ice cream—inspired by Norway, and Roald Dahl, of course!

WHAT YOU NEED TO DO

1 Whisk the double cream, condensed milk, and vanilla extract in the mixing bowl until it's as thick as slime.

2 Very lightly, stir in the caramel condensed milk.

3 Pour into the ice cream molds, and then add the sticks.

4 Put into the freezer overnight, making sure that the molds are totally flat.

5 Pop the ice cream out of the molds by dipping the molds in very hot water for a few seconds before removing the ice cream.

6 Sprinkle all over with the hazelnuts and raspberries.

7 Find the most comfortable spot in the house—and eat!

TOFFEE APPLES

FROM CHARLIE AND THE CHOCOLATE FACTORY

ILLUSTRATED BY STEVEN LENTON

MAKES ABOUT 12

YOU WILL NEED

EQUIPMENT

- melon scoop
- cocktail sticks
- small saucepan
- sugar thermometer
- large bowl containing water and ice cubes, kept in fridge

INGREDIENTS

- 4 eating apples
- ½ tbsp. water
- ½ cup caster sugar
- 1¾ tbsp. butter

WHAT YOU NEED TO DO

1 Using the melon scoop, scoop as many balls as possible from 3 apples. Each apple ball must have some skin on it.

2 Place a cocktail stick into the remaining skin left on each ball.

3 Get an adult to help you with this next part. Place the other ingredients into a saucepan and heat gently, stirring occasionally. Turn up the heat and boil to 160°C/325°F. The mixture will become a deep chestnut brown. Turn off the heat and allow bubbles to subside.

4 Remove the bowl of ice water from the fridge. Working as quickly as possible, dip the apples into the toffee one at a time. Rotate a few times to get an even coating and drop into the iced water for around 30 seconds.

5 Now stick the baby toffee apples into the remaining whole apple and continue until all the toffee is used up.

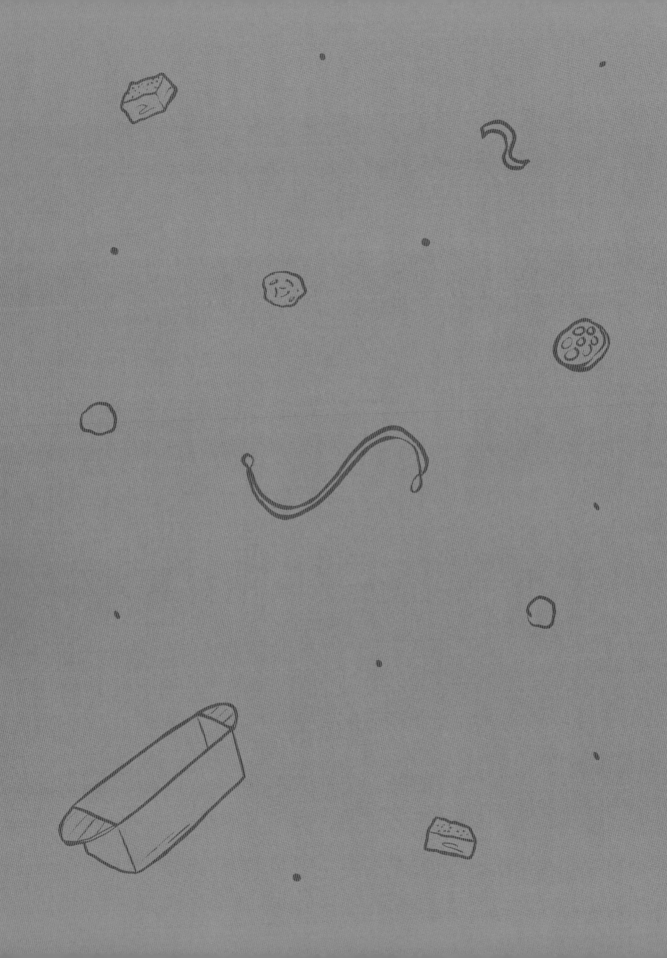

SWEET SNACKS

JELLIED GNATS

FROM JAMES AND THE GIANT PEACH

ILLUSTRATED BY
EMMA CHICHESTER CLARK

MAKES 30 SQUARES

YOU WILL NEED

EQUIPMENT

- saucepan
- plastic wrap
- 1-lb. loaf pan lined with lightly greased baking paper

INGREDIENTS

- 5 gelatin sheets
- ⅓ cup milk, chilled
- 2 cups double cream
- ⅓ cup caster sugar
- ½ tsp. vanilla paste
- zest from ½ lemon
- 1 tsp. chia seeds
- 1 tsp. black sesame seeds
- 1 tsp. poppy seeds

WHAT YOU NEED TO DO

1 Soak the gelatin sheets in the milk, in a bowl, until they are soft (this will take about a minute).

2 Mix the cream, caster sugar, vanilla paste, and lemon zest in a saucepan and stir slowly over medium heat to dissolve the sugar.

3 When the sugar is dissolved, and the mixture is nearly boiling, take it off the heat. Be careful because it will be very hot!

4 Pour the mixture onto the gelatin—make sure the adult you have selected is either standing right next to you or doing it for you.

5 Stir until the gelatin is dissolved. Cover the mixture with plastic wrap, and put into the fridge for 10 minutes. Then pour into the loaf pan. Sprinkle the seeds all over, and very carefully put in the fridge until set. This will take 1–2 hours.

6 Cut into squares and allow to come up to room temperature. These will also keep in the fridge (covered) for a couple of days.

WONKA-VITE

FROM **CHARLIE** AND THE **GREAT GLASS ELEVATOR**

ILLUSTRATED BY AXEL SCHEFFLER

MAKES 35

YOU WILL NEED

EQUIPMENT

- rolling pin
- 2 small saucepans
- small ice cube mold

INGREDIENTS

- 7 lemongrass stalks
- ⅔ cup caster sugar
- 1½ cups water
- 1 tbsp. water (to soak the gelatin)
- 3¼ tsp. gelatin powder
- a tiny bit of oil (this will need to be flavorless—anything apart from extra-virgin olive oil or toasted sesame oil is fine)
- 4 strawberries, chopped

WHAT YOU NEED TO DO

1   We're starting with the best bit. Get a rolling pin and bash all the lemongrass as hard as you can. This bruises it and helps release the flavor. Make sure you hit the lemongrass and not your fingers (they aren't an ingredient).

2 Put the bruised lemongrass in a saucepan with the sugar and water. Cook over medium heat for about 10 minutes until all the sugar is melted and the mixture has turned a very pale yellow. This is your lemongrass syrup.

3 While the lemongrass is cooking, put the tablespoon of water into the other small saucepan and sprinkle the gelatin into it. Allow the gelatin to absorb all the water. This will take about a minute, and it will look like there is no water left.

4 When the lemongrass syrup from step 2 is ready, take it off the heat. Carefully remove the lemongrass with a fork and throw it away, pour the syrup over the gelatin, and stir to dissolve. If the gelatin's not fully dissolved after a couple of minutes of stirring, put it on very low heat and stir. This should be done for as little time and with as little stirring as possible. Allow to cool.

5 Lightly grease the mold with the oil.

6 Put a few pieces of strawberry in each hole, and then slowly pour the cooled syrup to fill each one up to the surface. Pop into the fridge to set fully—this will take a couple of hours. Test the sweets gently with your finger to see if they're firm. If not, you'll need to put them back in the fridge.

7 When they are firm, remove from the fridge and loosen the edge of each one very gently with your finger and turn upside down. They should pop out quite easily.

Licorice
BOOTLACES
FROM BOY

ILLUSTRATED BY CHRIS WORMELL

This is one recipe that requires you to buy an ingredient not always available in the supermarket—licorice paste. But it will make LOADS more than this recipe, and it lasts for AGES.

MAKES 28 LACES

YOU WILL NEED

EQUIPMENT

- small saucepan
- whisk
- palette knife
- baking sheet, lightly greased

INGREDIENTS

- ⅓ cup water
- 6½ tsp. gelatin powder
- 1½ tbsp. molasses
- 1½ oz. licorice paste (you may need to order this online—please ask a parent to help!)
- ¼ tsp. black food coloring
- 1 tsp. salt
- ½ cup plain flour
- 1 small bag of jelly beans

WHAT YOU NEED TO DO

1 Put the water into a small saucepan and slowly sprinkle the gelatin powder into it. Then let it sit for about 5 minutes. This is called "letting it bloom."

2 Gently heat the gelatin and water mixture until it is liquid and clear. Make sure it doesn't get too hot and doesn't boil.

3 Add the molasses, licorice paste, food coloring, and salt. Melt the mixture over low heat.

4 Remove from the heat and whisk the flour into the mixture.

5 Put it back onto the heat and bring to a low boil, whisking constantly. It will thicken a lot!

6 With a palette knife, spread the mixture onto a baking sheet, on a flat surface, to a thickness of about $1/10$ in. Don't worry if you can't get it that thin—some laces can be thicker than others.

7 Now allow it to set until it feels firm enough to cut into strips (your laces). This will take about half an hour.

8 Cut the jelly beans in half lengthways and stick to the ends of the laces. The jelly beans are sticky on the inside, so they should attach quite well (if they don't, you can wet them very lightly).

WRIGGLE-SWEETS

FROM **CHARLIE** AND THE **CHOCOLATE FACTORY**

ILLUSTRATED BY LANE SMITH

MAKES LOTS

YOU WILL NEED

EQUIPMENT

- 4 containers to set the Wriggle-Sweets in (They need to be flat at the bottom and roughly 5 × 5 in., but the sweets can really be set in anything flat where they end up about ¼ in. high—large Tupperware containers are ideal.)
- 4 glasses
- small saucepan
- plastic wrap
- quite a lot of space in the fridge, as these need to chill for a couple of hours

INGREDIENTS

- 1 tsp. flavorless oil
- 4 different-colored fruit juices—3⅓ oz. of each
- 3⅓ oz. elderflower soda
- 3⅓ oz. elderflower syrup
- 4 tbsp. gelatin powder

WHAT YOU NEED TO DO

1   Very lightly grease the containers with the oil.

2   Pour the juices into the four glasses—one color for each glass.

3   Pour the elderflower soda and the syrup into the small saucepan and scatter the gelatin into the liquid. Leave for a couple of minutes, until all the liquid has been absorbed by the gelatin.

4   Put the saucepan over a very low heat and let the liquid completely melt, until it is clear. This will take about 4 minutes.

5   Divide the melted mixture equally between the four glasses of juice, and stir gently for about 20 seconds. Then pour each one into one of the four containers.

6   Cover the mixture with plastic wrap or a lid (making sure nothing is touching the surface of the liquid) and put in the fridge for a couple of hours, or until it's completely set, like a firm jelly.

7   When set, carefully loosen around the edges of each container with a knife so the mixture inside can easily come free. Then, using your fingers, slowly lift the mixture out of each container. Put each mixture on a board and cut into strips. These are your Wriggle-Sweets! They will keep for a couple of days in the fridge.

NISHNOBBLERS

FROM THE GIRAFFE AND THE PELLY AND ME

ILLUSTRATED BY QUENTIN BLAKE

Yummy with a big glass of milk!

MAKES 6

YOU WILL NEED

EQUIPMENT

- heat-resistant bowl
- saucepan
- 12 × 10–in. sheet of Bubble Wrap
- pastry brush
- 3 in. cookie cutter

INGREDIENTS

- ⅔ cup good-quality dark chocolate
- ⅔ cup good-quality white chocolate

WHAT YOU NEED TO DO

Nishnobblers are made from tempered chocolate. Tempering is when you mix melted and solid chocolate together to make it shinier and more manageable. It is an indispensable skill to have in life, and you learn how to do it right here! Once you've got the hang of it, you'll be able to create masterful chocolate constructions to rival Willy Wonka's.

1   Melt about ½ cup of the dark chocolate in a heat-resistant bowl on the defrost setting in the microwave or over a saucepan of simmering water (for more instructions on melting chocolate, see page 116). When it is melted, stir in the remaining chocolate until it's all smooth.

2   Use the pastry brush to paint over the Bubble Wrap with the melted chocolate and place it in the fridge for 15 minutes.

3   Temper the white chocolate in the same way. (White chocolate melts faster than dark chocolate, so you may want to let it cool a little before you start painting.) Spread it over the dark chocolate already painted on the Bubble Wrap. Chill for 15 minutes.

4   Carefully peel the Bubble Wrap away from the chocolate and cut it into rounds with the pastry cutter.

HAIR CREAM

FROM **CHARLIE** AND THE **CHOCOLATE FACTORY**

ILLUSTRATED BY ALEX SCARFE

MAKES 2

YOU WILL NEED

EQUIPMENT

- saucepan
- tongs
- small food processor
- piping bag and star nozzle
- vegetable peeler

This will taste a whole lot better than actual hair cream.

INGREDIENTS

- 4 apples (your favorite kind), with the stems attached
- ½ cup caster sugar
- 4 oz. water
- 4 tbsp. crème fraîche
- 2 chocolate buttons

WHAT YOU NEED TO DO

1 Remove the stems from the apples (keep the stems, as you'll need them for later). Peel two of the apples and take out the cores (get an adult to help you with this bit), then cut each one into 12 wedges.

2 You'll need the adult for this step too. Put the sugar and water into a saucepan over high heat. You're going to make caramel, which is delicious but gets very hot. Cook the sugar until it turns a caramel color. This will take roughly 10 minutes, but keep an eye on it, because it might take less time. Don't stir, because it will crystallize.

3 When the caramel is cooked, add 20 apple wedges to the saucepan. Continue cooking but on a low heat, until the apple is very soft. Use tongs to take the wedges out of the caramel and put onto a plate to cool. When they are cooled sufficiently, so they are warm rather than hot, put into the food processor.

4 Then put the remaining 4 apple wedges into the saucepan on a low heat and cook until very soft and golden.

5 While they are cooking, process the 20 wedges of apple in the food processor until smooth. Transfer to a bowl to cool. When cool, add the crème fraîche and mix.

6 When the rest of the apple wedges are cooked, use the tongs to transfer to a plate and let them cool completely. Keep the caramel on a very low heat so it remains soft, because you'll need it later.

7 Now comes the fun bit! Put the cooked apple wedges over the top of the remaining 2 apples to look like someone's hair. You can decide on the style, or look at the photo for inspiration.

8 Put the apple and crème fraîche mix into a piping bag with the star nozzle already in and pipe the mixture (the hair cream) over the top of the caramelized wedges (the hair). Stick the chocolate buttons (eyes) and the stems (nose and mouth) on the apple, using the leftover caramel as glue. Then you're good to go!

WHOOPSEY-SPLUNKERS

FROM THE
BFG

ILLUSTRATED BY IAN BECK

MAKES 12 (and they keep for AGES in the fridge)

YOU WILL NEED

EQUIPMENT

- food processor

INGREDIENTS

- 5 dates (pits removed)
- 1 oz. oats
- 1 oz. toasted almonds (for advice on how to toast nuts, please see page 114)
- 3½ tbsp. peanut, almond, or cashew butter
- ½ tsp. vanilla extract
- 1 tsp. lemon zest
- pinch of salt
- 1 oz. cashews
- ¾ cup dried coconut

WHAT YOU NEED TO DO

1 Soak the dates in hot water for 5 minutes and then remove them (discard the liquid).

2 Put everything apart from the dried coconut into the food processor.

3 Pulse until everything comes together like a ball of cement.

4 Take tablespoon-sized amounts of the mixture, and shape into balls.

5 Put the dried coconut into a small bowl and toss each ball around in it until completely coated. They are now ready to eat!

VITA-WONK

FROM **CHARLIE** AND THE **GREAT GLASS ELEVATOR**

ILLUSTRATED BY MINI GREY

MAKES 8

YOU WILL NEED

EQUIPMENT

- ice cube tray or silicone mold with round holes
- pastry brush

INGREDIENTS

- a tiny bit of oil (this will need to be flavorless—anything apart from extra-virgin olive oil or toasted sesame oil is fine)
- ⅔ cup dark chocolate, chopped
- 1 bag of M&Ms
- ⅓ cup white chocolate
- 24 mini marshmallows
- gold luster powder (optional)
- edible gold glitter (optional)

WHAT YOU NEED TO DO

1   Very lightly grease the ice cube tray with the flavorless oil.

2   Melt the dark chocolate in a heat-resistant bowl in the microwave on a defrost setting, or by putting in a bowl over a saucepan of simmering water (see more information on melting chocolate on page 116). Now brush the inside of each cube in the tray with the melted chocolate. When you have done this once, put the tray in the freezer or fridge until completely set—this should take between 2 and 5 minutes—then brush on another layer of melted chocolate. You need to do this four times, and you should have some chocolate left over.

3   When the final layer is painted, put the ice cube tray back in the freezer for another 5 minutes.

4   Chop up the M&Ms and white chocolate into small chunks and get the marshmallows ready.

5   Take the ice cube tray out of the fridge or freezer and let it sit at room temperature for another 5 minutes.

6   Very carefully, using the tip of a small sharp knife (this should be an adult's job!), loosen the top of the chocolate in each tray. Turn over and carefully tap each one out of the tray. If they break very slightly, it's important not to panic! The leftover melted chocolate is like glue, so you can just piece them back together.

7 Fill half of the chocolate shells with the M&Ms, white chocolate, and marshmallows. Take your leftover melted chocolate, and dip the edge of an empty chocolate shell into it. Fix this sticky edge to one of your filled chocolate shells so that you end up with one whole chocolate ball.

8 When each chocolate ball is completely set, brush with the luster powder and sprinkle with the edible glitter (if using).

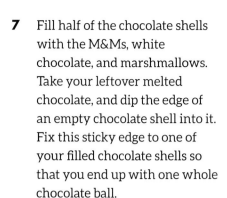

9 You can either eat the Vita-Wonk straight away or, if you fancy it, heat up some milk and pop a Vita-Wonk in to make a scrumptious drink!

Fried
SNOWBALLS

FROM **JAMES** AND GIANT THE **PEACH**

ILLUSTRATED BY LANE SMITH

These Fried Snowballs should definitely come with a warning. Once you've eaten one, it's very hard to stop!

MAKES 24

YOU WILL NEED

EQUIPMENT

- food processor
- small saucepan or heat-resistant bowl
- clean, damp tea towel
- rolling pin
- baking paper, lightly greased
- 2-in. round cookie cutter
- baking tray (with raised edges)
- plastic wrap
- wide, deep saucepan
- slotted spoon
- paper towels

INGREDIENTS

- 1¾ cups plain flour
- pinch of salt
- 1 tsp. fast-action yeast, dried
- 2¼ tbsp. cold butter, chopped into cubes
- 5 oz. milk
- ¼ cup caster sugar
- 2 egg yolks
- 2 cups vegetable oil, or enough to fill the pan to 2 or 2½ in. deep
- 4 tbsp. powdered sugar, sprinkled onto a plate

WHAT YOU NEED TO DO

1   Sift the flour and salt into a bowl, then add the yeast.

2   Put the mixture into the food processor. Add the cold butter cubes and process for around a minute, until the mixture resembles small bread crumbs.

3   Warm the milk on the stove or in a heat-resistant bowl in the microwave for 30 seconds, until just warm. Mix together the warm milk, caster sugar, and egg yolks.

4   Pour the flour mix into a large bowl and slowly add the milk and egg liquid. Mix until it forms a smooth, soft dough. It will be quite wet.

5   Leave it covered with a clean, damp tea towel in a warm place until it's doubled in size. This will take about an hour.

6   Knead the dough for about 10 minutes. (This is a very sticky dough, so dust the work surface and your hands with flour!) Roll out onto a large, lightly greased piece of baking paper until it's ½ in. thick and roughly 8 × 8 in. in size. Dip the cookie cutter in flour and cut out as many discs as you can. Then reroll the remaining dough and repeat until you have twenty-four. Roll each disc into a round snowball, then put these onto a baking tray and place plastic wrap over them, ensuring the plastic wrap doesn't touch the snowballs. Leave until they have doubled in size again—this will take 45 minutes to an hour.

7   Get an adult to help you with this step. Add around 2–2½ in. of oil to your saucepan. Heat the oil to around 180°C/350°F, or until the oil starts to bubble.

8   Drop each ball carefully into the saucepan and deep-fry for 1–2 minutes, until golden brown and cooked all the way through. (One side will go golden before the other, so use the slotted spoon to flip it over and cook the other side for the same amount of time.) When cooked, very briefly drain on a paper towel. When they are cool, roll each ball in the powdered sugar. Now they're ready to eat!

Crispy
WASP STINGS
on a Piece of Buttered Toast

FROM **JAMES** AND **GIANT PEACH** THE

ILLUSTRATED BY QUENTIN BLAKE

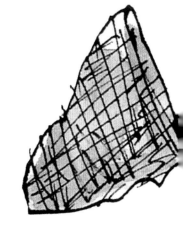

MAKES 16

YOU WILL NEED

EQUIPMENT

- small round cookie cutter
- baking sheet lined with baking paper
- spatula

INGREDIENTS

For the buttered toast

- 4¼ tbsp. softened butter
- ½ tsp. ground cinnamon
- 4 slices of white bread

For the wasp stings

- ¾ cup dried coconut
- 3½ tbsp. powdered sugar, sifted
- 3 tsp. clear honey or golden syrup
- grated zest of ¼ lemon

WHAT YOU NEED TO DO

1 Work the butter and cinnamon together until thoroughly mixed.

2 Use the cookie cutter to cut four discs out of each slice of bread and set aside.

3 Spread three-quarters of the dried coconut onto the baking sheet and cover with the sifted powdered sugar.

4 Place the baking tray under your oven's broiler until the sugar begins to caramelize (it will happen very quickly). Then use the spatula to turn over the coconut, before popping it back under the broiler again. Repeat until all the sides of the coconut are caramelized.

5 Place the coconut mixture in a bowl and add the honey and lemon zest, then mix well.

6 Add the remaining coconut.

7 Add the bread discs to the baking tray and toast them on both sides under the broiler.

8 Spread with the cinnamon butter and top with the crispy wasp stings.

Perfect birthday party food!

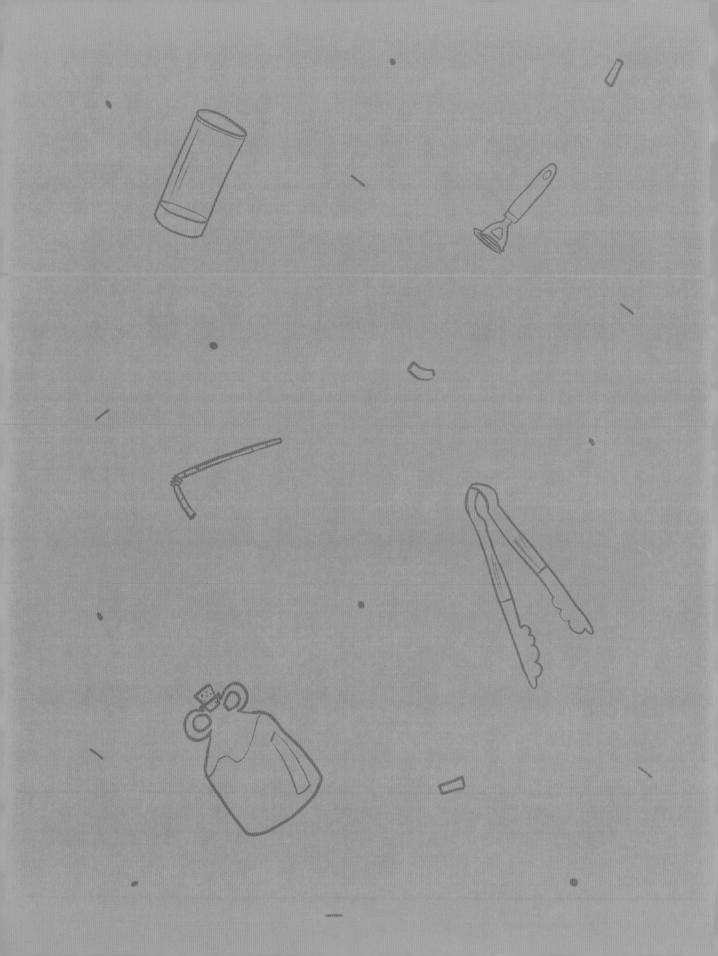

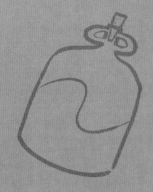

DRINKS

FROTHBLOWERS

FROM
THE GIRAFFE AND THE PELLY AND ME

ILLUSTRATED BY STEVEN LENTON

INGREDIENTS

- sprinkles (any kind you like the look of)
- ⅔ cup dark chocolate
- 1 very ripe banana
- 4 generous scoops of salted-caramel ice cream
- ½ cup milk (any kind of milk will do)
- 2 tsp. almond butter (or any kind of nut butter)

MAKES ABOUT 14 OZ.

YOU WILL NEED

EQUIPMENT

- small, shallow bowl
- heat-resistant bowl
- glasses or mini milk bottles (You can use anything you like. This recipe is enough for 6 small glasses, so if you choose larger ones, it will make fewer, and smaller ones will make more.)
- blender
- lots of paper or metal straws

WHAT YOU NEED TO DO

1 Put the sprinkles into a small, shallow bowl.

2 Break the chocolate into small pieces and put into a heat-resistant bowl. Melt the chocolate in the microwave on the defrost setting for 2 minutes at a time, stirring after each 2 minutes until the chocolate is completely melted. Alternatively, you can use a glass bowl and pan of hot water to melt the chocolate. (For techniques on how to melt chocolate, please see page 116.)

3 Now you have to work fast! Dip the top of each glass or bottle into the melted chocolate, so it drips down and over the sides, and then dip it into the sprinkles.

4 Put all the other ingredients into a blender and blend for about 30 seconds.

5 Carefully pour the mixture (the Frothblower) into the glasses, put the straws in, and drink!

BEAN'S CIDER

FROM FANTASTIC MR. FOX

ILLUSTRATED BY EMILY WOODARD

MAKES 1 SERVING

YOU WILL NEED

EQUIPMENT

- peeler
- apple corer
- food processor or blender
- sieve
- small saucepan

INGREDIENTS

- 4 apples—a sweet variety, such as Fuji or Gala
- 1 lime, juiced
- 2 tbsp. light muscovado sugar
- 1 cinnamon stick, broken into 3 pieces
- small carton of apple juice (optional)

WHAT YOU NEED TO DO

1   Peel and core the apples.

2   Place the apples in the food processor or blender with the lime juice and purée for 4 minutes.

3   Push the purée through the sieve into a small saucepan.

4   Add the muscovado sugar and the broken cinnamon stick.

5   Heat gently while stirring.

6   Push through the sieve again—if it is too thick, add some apple juice.

7   Serve in a glass and enjoy!

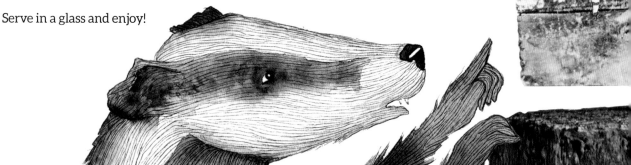

FIZZWINKLES

FROM THE GIRAFFE AND THE PELLY AND ME

ILLUSTRATED BY EMILY WOODARD

These fruits are just a guide—if you don't like any of them, choose ones you do like. But ideally, you want them to be all different colors.

MAKES 1 GLASS

YOU WILL NEED

EQUIPMENT

- blender
- 2 ice cube trays (any kind)
- paper or metal straws

INGREDIENTS

- 750 ml bottle sparkling elderflower soda
- 1 small pack watermelon pieces, or ¼ small watermelon, cut into pieces
- 1 pink grapefruit, cut into pieces
- 3 kiwi fruits, cut into slices
- 1 cantaloupe melon (orange melon), cut into slices
- 4 blueberries
- 4 raspberries
- edible rose petals (optional)

WHAT YOU NEED TO DO

1 Blend each type of fruit separately with a teaspoon of the elderflower soda (apart from the berries, which you need to leave whole). This will give you four different-color purées.

2 Pour the purées into the ice cube tray (as many holes as possible), being sure to keep each purée separate. Put the berries in separate holes, and fill it up with the rest of the elderflower soda.

3 Pop the trays into the freezer and freeze for a few hours until the mixtures are completely solid.

4 Pop the cubes out of the trays.

5 Fill one large glass all the way to the top with the cubes.

6 Then fill up the rest of the glass with the elderflower soda. Sprinkle with the rose petals, if using.

7 Add your straw and enjoy. As the ice melts, the flavors will change!

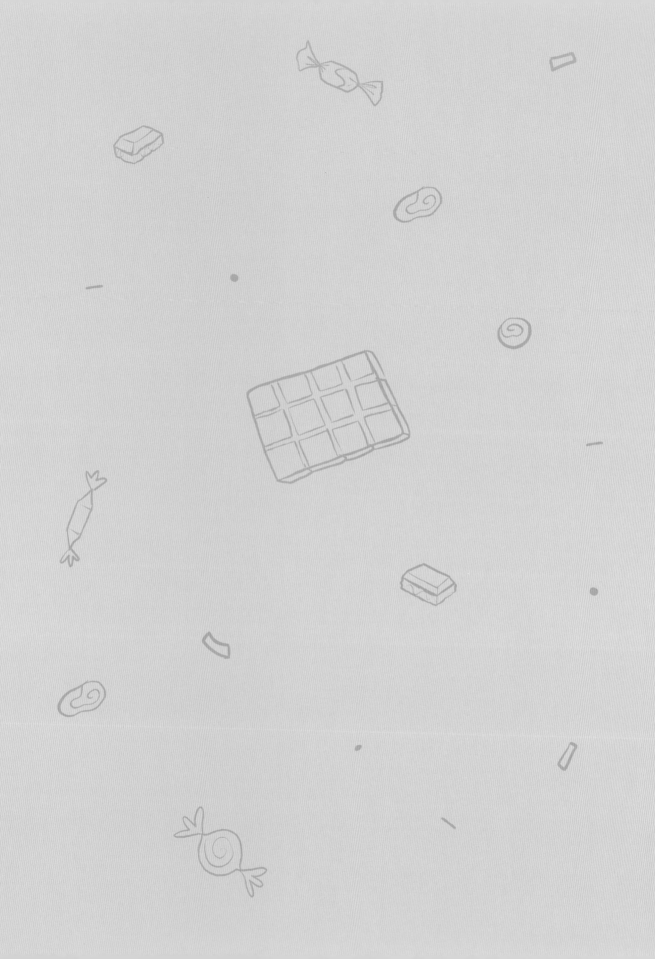

A HISTORY OF CHOCOLATE

Roald Dahl had a passion for chocolate. He believed that every child in every school—as well as learning the dates of battles and all the kings and queens of the world—should learn about the history of chocolate and the bars and treats that have been delighting children (and grown-ups) for the last hundred years.

We have created a chocolate timeline especially for this book, with the dates of when each chocolate bar was invented.

We hope you enjoy!

"I would get rid of the history teacher and get a chocolate teacher instead."
—Roald Dahl

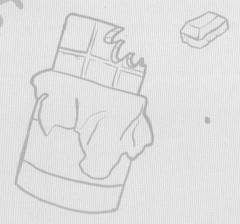

1905
Cadbury's
DAIRY MILK

1908
BOURNVILLE

1920
Cadbury's
**DAIRY MILK
FLAKE**

1932
MARS

1926
Cadbury's
**FRUIT
AND NUT**

1929
Fry's
CRUNCHIE

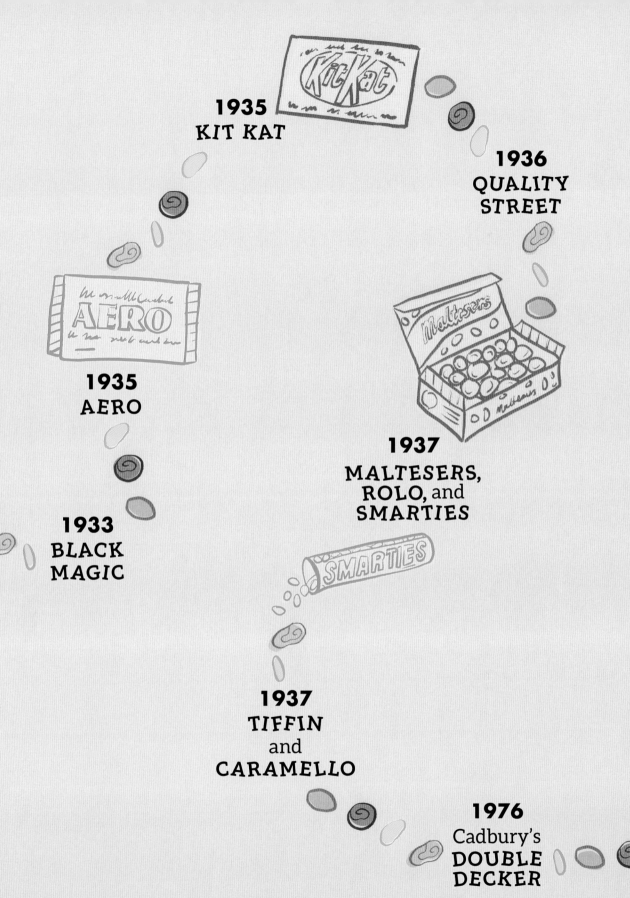

1935
KIT KAT

1936
QUALITY
STREET

1935
AERO

1937
MALTESERS,
ROLO, and
SMARTIES

1933
BLACK
MAGIC

1937
TIFFIN
and
CARAMELLO

1976
Cadbury's
DOUBLE
DECKER

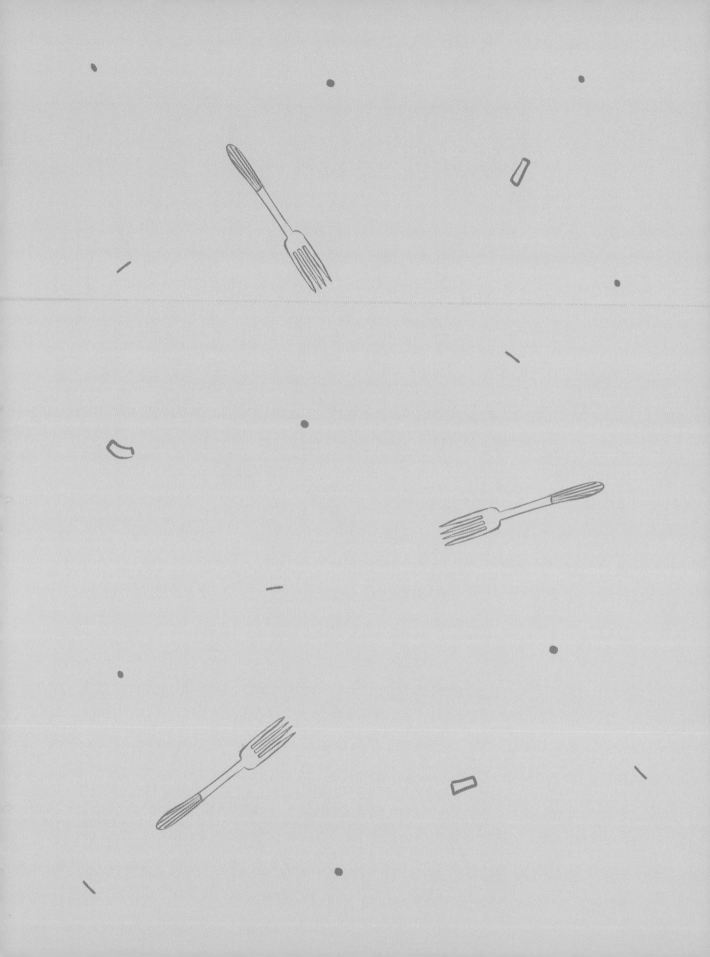

EQUIPMENT
AND
ESSENTIAL
INGREDIENTS

ESSENTIAL EQUIPMENT

MIXING BOWLS
It's good to keep a
few sizes on hand.

BOWLS
Sometimes these will need to be heat
resistant, which means they won't
melt when heated up! Check each recipe
to see whether your bowl needs to be
heat resistant and what size of bowl
you might need.

WEIGHING SCALES

PLATES

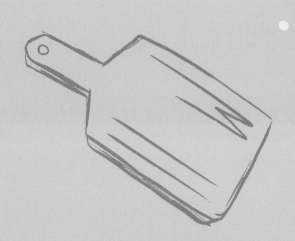

CUTTING BOARD

FRYING PAN

OVEN

FORK

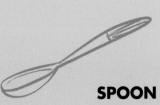

SPOON

FRIDGE

FREEZER

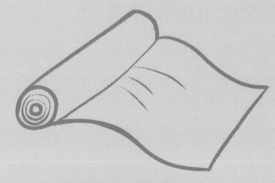

BAKING PAPER
This should be nonstick and is used so food doesn't stick to the bottom of your baking tray!

BAKING TRAY

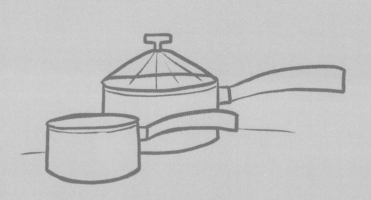

SAUCEPANS
These could be small, medium, or large, depending on the recipe, and they will sometimes need a lid.

SCISSORS

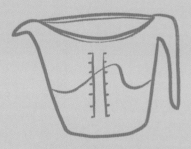

MEASURING CUP

FOIL

PAPER TOWELS

EQUIPMENT NEEDED FOR SOME RECIPES

MELON SCOOP

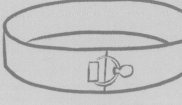

CAKE PANS

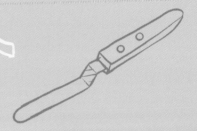

SMALL PALETTE KNIFE
(Or you can always use
a blunt butter knife.)

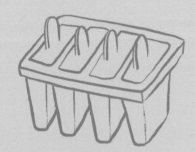

**ICE CREAM OR ICE POP
MOLDS**

ICE CUBE TRAYS

WHISK
You can use an electric whisk for some
recipes if you want to, because it will
make the whisking faster and easier!
For a few recipes (Swudge, for instance),
an electric hand mixer is essential.

JAM JARS

GLASSES

TUPPERWARE

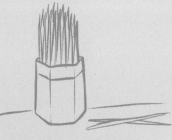

COCKTAIL STICKS

PEELER

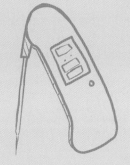

APPLE CORER

**DIGITAL AND SUGAR
THERMOMETERS**
(These are optional,
and there are other ways
of checking if something
is hot enough.)

SPATULA

TONGS

ROASTING PAN

COOKIE CUTTERS
(We suggest you buy a pack of
these if you're baking regularly.)

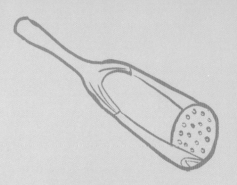

POTATO MASHER

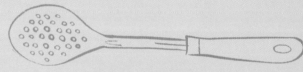

PASTRY BRUSH

TEA TOWEL

SLOTTED SPOON

WOODEN SKEWERS

COLANDER

PIPING BAGS
(See the piping method on
page 106 for the different types
of piping bags that can be used.)

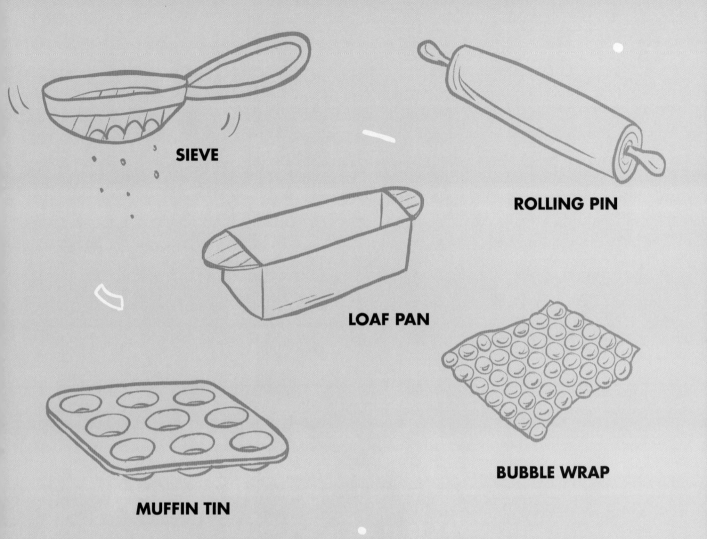

SIEVE

ROLLING PIN

LOAF PAN

BUBBLE WRAP

MUFFIN TIN

BASIC INGREDIENTS

SALT AND PEPPER

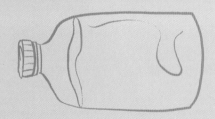

OIL
(There are a few different types of oil used in this book. Olive oil is most often used in savory food—usually pasta or other European dishes. Vegetable oil is known as a neutral oil. This means it's good for when you don't want to taste the oil, and it is sometimes used in sweet dishes.)

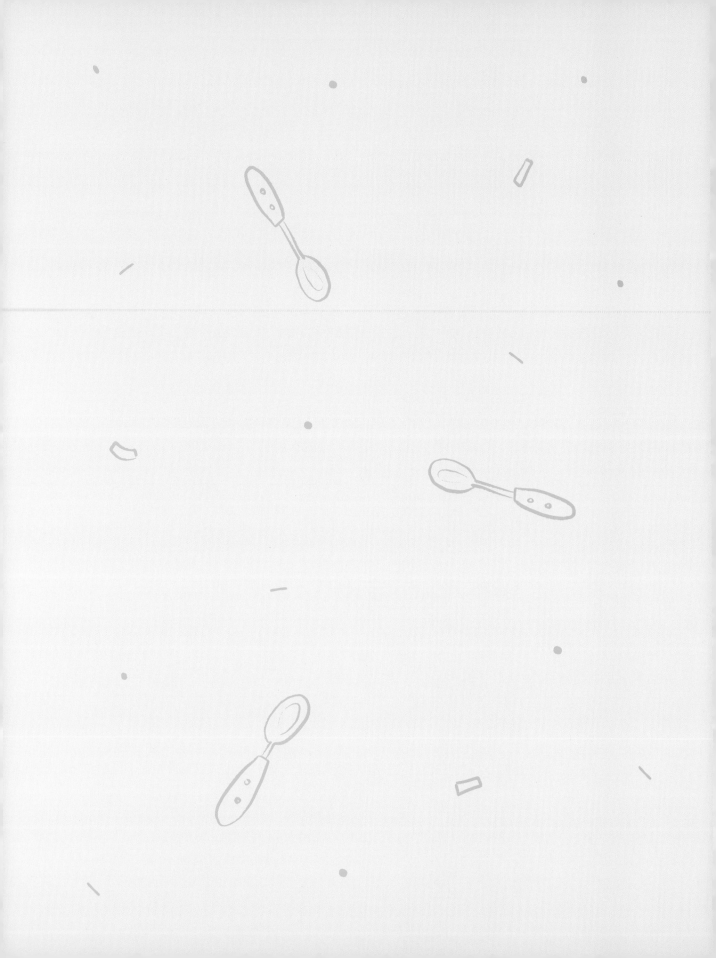

A GUIDE TO USING EQUIPMENT

FOOD PROCESSORS

TYPES

You can buy quite a few different types of food processors, but generally their main differences are size. Some recipes may ask for a small one and some for a large one, but you can just use whatever you have available. The reason some ask you to use a bigger one is that the mixture is a large amount, but you can always process in two or three smaller batches.

USAGE

Food processors are usually used for chopping solid foods into small pieces. They can be used to chop individual things, or sometimes a few different items might get chopped together—this means they all get mixed at the same time, which might be needed for a particular recipe.

BLENDERS

TYPES

You can also buy different types of blenders. Some are in the classic jug style, but you can also get stick blenders or high-speed blenders, which do the same job as a normal blender but in different ways! With high-speed blenders, you might need to blend your food in batches.

USAGE

Blenders are usually used for processing solids into purées, pastes, or liquid form—like a soup. Always make sure whatever you're blending isn't hot, to prevent any explosions!

PIPING BAG

There are a few recipes in this book that ask you to fill and use a piping bag, and there are a few different ways to do this. We use a nozzle in a piping bag when we want whatever we're piping to look pretty and decorative. For this, you put the nozzle into the bag first, before cutting the end of the bag and pushing the end of the nozzle through (cutting a bit more of the bag if needed). It's a good idea to ask your grown-up to do this for you, as it can be a bit tricky!

For the Scarlet Scorchdroppers recipe, you fill the piping bag without the nozzle because the piping is allowed to be a bit messier for this one. Putting the bag into a glass helps it stay upright while you pour in the liquid chocolate.

SPOONS (TBSP./TSP.)

It can be worth investing in a set of measuring spoons, especially when it comes to baking. If you see "1 tbsp," this means "1 tablespoon," and "1 tsp." means "1 teaspoon."

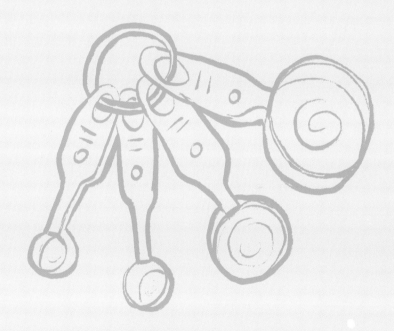

SLOTTED SPOON

This is a large spoon, usually metal, that has holes in it and is used for draining.

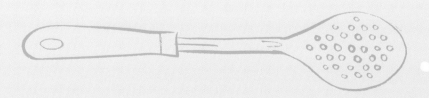

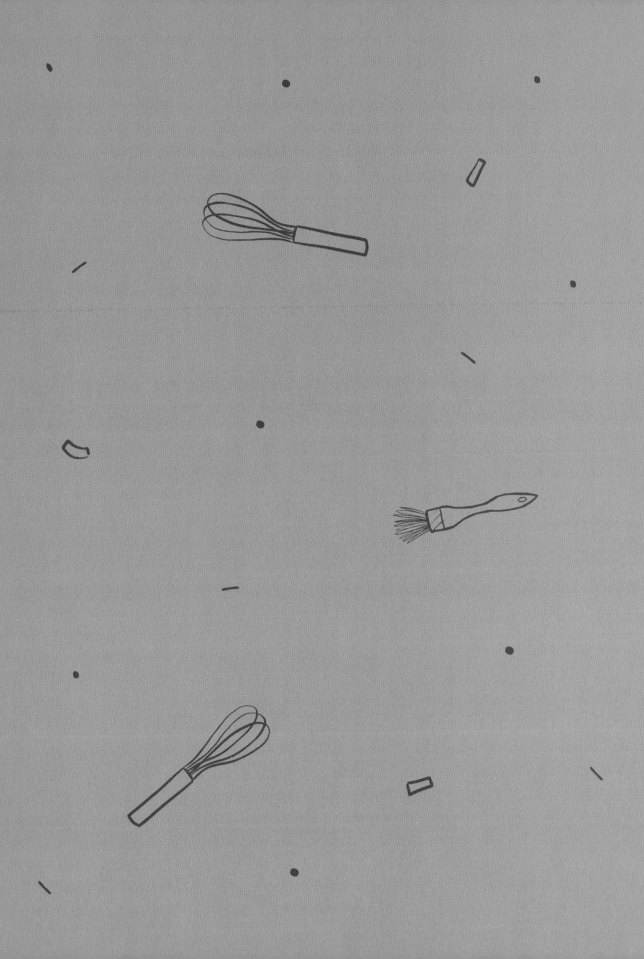

A GUIDE TO COOKING METHODS

DRAINING

This is when you separate a solid from a liquid, usually using a sieve or colander. In the Dandyprats recipe, to drain the macaroni, you put a sieve or colander into the sink and carefully (ask an adult for help with this!) tip the pan over the sieve/colander, so you're just left with your lovely cooked pasta and the water has been poured away. Sometimes you can also drain onto paper towels on a plate—like in the Hot Noodles recipe. This is for when we want to dry things that are a bit more delicate.

STRAINING

This is very similar to draining but usually means you're taking something *out* of a liquid, and for this you might use a slotted spoon.

BLANCHING

Blanching is when you cook something very quickly in a hot liquid, like boiling water, usually only for a few seconds or minutes. This method is used when the food doesn't need much cooking or you're going to cook it again in a different way later.

SIFTING

This is when you shake powdered foods like flour or powdered sugar through a sieve to remove any lumps before adding to your recipe.

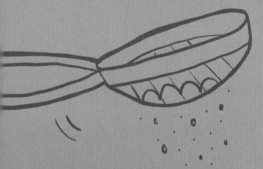

ZESTING

This is when you remove the very outer part of citrus fruits—like lemons, limes, and oranges—and use this to flavor a recipe. You can do this on the fine side of a cheese grater, or you can buy a special zester. (But it's better to let your grown-ups do any zesting so you don't cut yourself!) Always be careful not to zest the white part underneath the outer part (the pith), as this isn't very tasty.

REMOVING ICE CUBES FROM TRAYS

If you're using plastic ice cube trays, the easiest way to remove the ice cubes is to lightly run some warm water over the base of the trays. Then they should pop out more easily. If you're using silicone ice trays, just gently wiggle them and the ice cubes will come out.

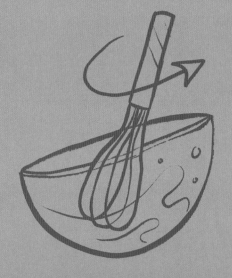

BEATING EGGS

This is when you use either a small whisk or a fork to mix eggs together, moving your hand in a circular motion until the yolks and whites are well combined.

WHISKING EGG WHITES

When a recipe asks you to whisk egg whites until stiff, this means using a whisk (ideally an electric one) to beat them until they are firm. When you think they are stiff enough, dip your whisk in and out of the egg-white mixture and—if ready—the beaten egg whites should stand up on their own.

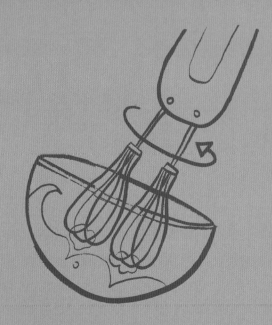

HARD-BOILING EGGS

To hard-boil an egg, add it to a pan of boiling water and cook for 8 minutes. Use a slotted spoon to carefully remove the egg and put straight into a bowl of really cold water (with ice if possible) and leave for 10 minutes or until the egg is cold. Then remove from the water and carefully peel off the shell.

BRUSHING WITH EGG WASH

This is when you use a fork to mix an egg yolk in a small bowl (sometimes with milk, like in the Gumtwizzlers recipe) until smooth. Then you use a small brush to apply it over things like puff pastry so that when it's finished baking, it'll have a lovely shine!

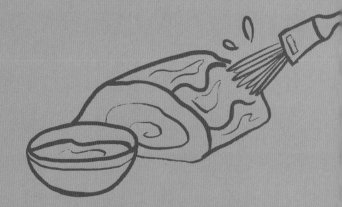

BRINGING TO A BOIL

This is when you heat a liquid, such as water, in a saucepan over medium-high heat. When the bubbles start to jump around really fast, the liquid is now boiling.

COOKING PASTA

When cooking pasta, like spaghetti, it's always best to follow the instructions on the package, because different brands might have different timings.

PEELING

Sometimes you might be asked to peel vegetables. The easiest way to do this is to hold whatever you're peeling on a cutting board and use your other hand to carefully peel, using a peeler (making sure to keep any fingers out of the way). Always get an adult to help you so you don't get cut.

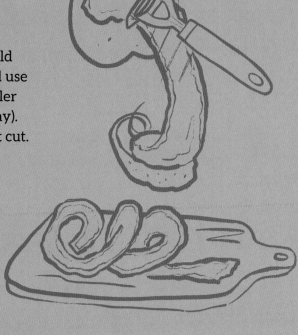

GRATING

This is when you use a grater (either a cheese grater or a handheld one) to grate cheese or vegetables into thin strands.

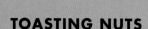

TOASTING NUTS

To toast nuts on the stove, add them to a dry frying pan on medium-low heat and let them toast all over for 4–5 minutes, making sure they don't burn. You can stir them with a wooden spoon or spatula to make sure they're evenly toasted.

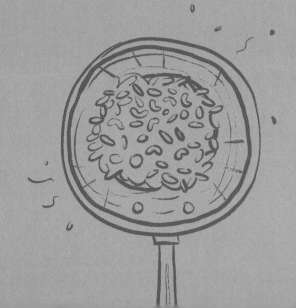

KNEADING

When kneading dough, like in the Fried Snowballs recipe, make your hands into open fists and use the heel of your right one (near your wrist) to push the dough away from you. Roll it back toward you, then do the same thing with your other hand. Keep repeating until your dough is nice and smooth.

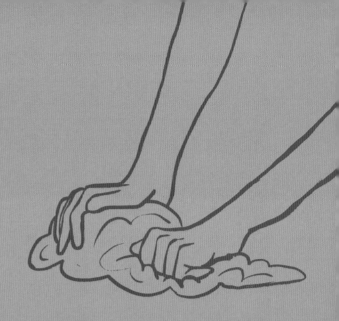

POWDERED GELATIN OR GELATIN SHEETS

There are two types of gelatin used in this book. Powdered gelatin should always be scattered evenly over a cold liquid and left to absorb for 5–10 minutes before heating. Gelatin sheets have to be left to soak for 5–10 minutes or until softened, before being added to a warmed liquid.

OILING FOIL

Dip a pastry brush into some oil and lightly brush over the foil. Or you can do the same technique using a piece of scrunched-up paper towel.

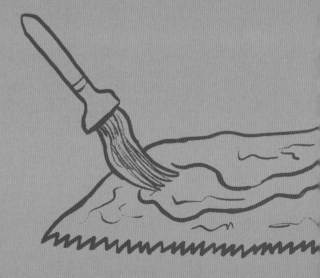

MELTING CHOCOLATE

There are two ways to melt chocolate, but whichever one you choose, always make sure there's an adult present! You could break the chocolate into small chunks, add it to a microwavable bowl, and put it in the microwave, on defrost, for 20 seconds. Remove from the microwave and stir, then put back in for another 20 seconds. Keep doing this a few times until melted.

The other way is to put a little bit of water in a saucepan, then add the broken-up chocolate to a bowl, which should fit snugly into the saucepan, with the top of the bowl poking out. Just make sure the water never touches the bottom of the bowl. Heat the saucepan and bowl on really low heat, stirring a lot, until the chocolate is melted.

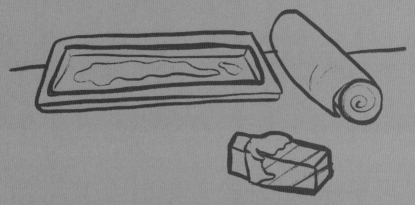

GREASING

Sometimes a recipe will ask you to grease a baking tray or grease baking paper.
This just means taking a little bit of melted butter or vegetable oil and spreading
it all over the tray or paper, so whatever is going on top won't stick.

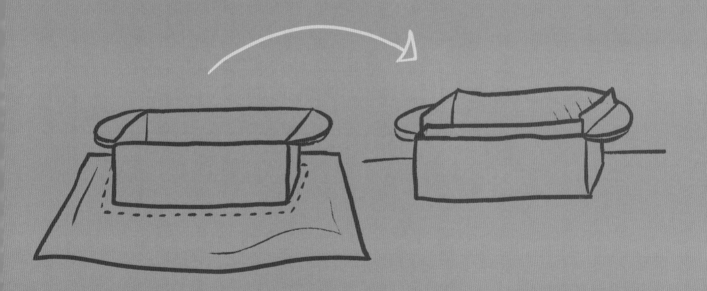

LINING A LOAF PAN

You can buy loaf pan liners that are already in the shape of a loaf pan, but if you
want to line them yourself, the best thing to do is put the loaf pan on top of some baking
paper and cut it into a rectangle shape 6 in. bigger than the loaf pan on all sides.
Grease the inside of the loaf pan. Make a diagonal cut from each corner of the baking paper
inward (about 2 in.), then push the paper into the loaf pan, making sure it's also
up the sides, carefully cutting off any paper if there's too much sticking up.

CHOPPING

There are a few different types of chopping in this book. "Finely chopped" means trying to get the pieces of food as small as possible with a knife. "Roughly chopped" means you can chop in bigger pieces.

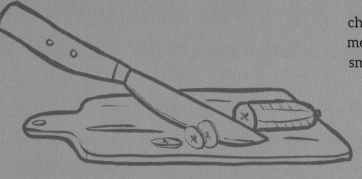

SWEATING

This is the gentle heating of vegetables in a little oil or butter, with frequent stirring and turning to ensure that any liquid will evaporate.

SAUTÉING

This just means to fry something for a few minutes, stirring as it cooks.

CRUSHING GARLIC

There are a few ways you can do this. Always peel your garlic and throw away the paper skins first. Then you can either use a garlic crusher or just chop the garlic up into very small pieces. If you want to use a small food processor, this is fine too!

MAKING STOCK

Some supermarkets sell ready-made stock.
Otherwise you can buy stock cubes or little stock jars.
Just follow the package instructions to make as much
stock as the recipe needs.

SEASONING WITH SALT AND PEPPER

When a recipe asks you to season with salt and pepper, this
simply means add a little pinch of each and taste the food. Does it
taste salty enough for you? If not, add a tiny bit more. Same with
the pepper. Remember you can add more but you can't take
away, so always start with small amounts!

ACKNOWLEDGMENTS

On behalf of Roald Dahl's Marvellous Children's Charity, I wish to thank all the illustrators who have made this book possible by filling it with a feast of visual humor. A big thank-you also to Lori Newman for inventing these wondercrump recipes; Jan Baldwin for ingenious photography; and Sarah Murray for doing the typing and being constantly fed during the experimental stage of the recipes! I also want to thank her for endless time arranging and placing everything in the correct order, thus enabling this book to be created. Also, I would like to thank Hannah Summers for the arduous task of testing all the recipes and creating a chocolate tree; my editor Tom Rawlinson for his enthusiastic support; and designer Katy Finch.

Last and by no means least, I thank Roald, my fantastic late husband, without whose inspiration this book would never have happened.

Felicity Dahl

Founder of Roald Dahl's Marvellous Children's Charity

YOUR RECIPE NOTES

SIZZLING SAUSAGES

FROM THE ENORMOUS CROCODILE

An extra-special, very simple recipe, inspired by the ending of The Enormous Crocodile

MAKES ANY NUMBER!

YOU WILL NEED

EQUIPMENT

- frying pan
- barbecue fork/tongs

INGREDIENTS

- 1 tsp. vegetable oil
- as many sausages as you would like—they can be any kind!

WHAT YOU NEED TO DO

1 Pour the vegetable oil into your frying pan. Place on a campfire, a grill, or your stove at home, and heat the oil for 10 seconds or so. (Make sure your adult helps you with this.)

2 Add the sausages, and cook for 10–12 minutes, turning them every few minutes. They will soon be sizzling!

3 Ask an adult to help you check that the sausages are cooked through. (There shouldn't be any pink color inside the sausages when you cut them open.)

4 You can serve them inside buns (maybe with some salad), as part of a breakfast, or just on their own!